Boost Your Interview Test Performance

Increase Your Chances of Climbing The Corporate Ladder

D&B PUBLISHING
www.dandbpublishing.com

Philip Carter

First published in 2005 by D&B Publishing,
PO Box 18, Hassocks, West Sussex BN6 9WR.

British Library Cataloguing-in-Publication Data
A catalogue record for this book is avalable
from the British Library.

ISBN 1-904468-18-7

All sales enquiries should be directed to:
D&B Publishing, PO Box 18, Hassocks,
West Sussex BN6 9WR, UK
Tel: 01273 834680, Fax: 01273 831629,
e-mail: info@dandbpublishing.com,
website: www.dandbpublishing.com

Cover Design by Horatio Monteverde.
Illustrations and typesetting by Mora Monteverde.
Production by Navigator Guides.
Printed and bound in the U.S.A. by Versa Press Inc.

Contents

Introduction

In order to get a foot on the corporate ladder it is first of all necessary to secure a position within a company, and this usually involves attending one or several job interviews, many of which incorporate psychometric testing as part of the selection process in addition to the usual face to face interview.

As defined by The British Psychological Society a psychometric test is an instrument designed to produce a quantitive assessment of some psychological attribute or attributes. Such tests are, in other words, a standard method of measuring one's ability, as accurately as it is scientifically possible to do so. A meaning of the word metric is measure, and psych means mind.

The incorporation of this form of testing provides the employer with an accurate assessment of whether an individual is able to do the required job and whether the person's character is suited to the work.

The purpose of this book is to familiarise readers with the type of psychometric tests given by employers to prospective employees, and thus increase their chances of achieving a successful outcome when attending one of the many job interviews that incorporate this type of testing. Such tests measure aptitude, intelligence quotient (IQ), creativity, problem solving, perception and personality. They identify not only candidates who appear to be well suited to the job on offer but also those who display the potential for developing their career within the company and achieving success in a business environment.

Because all the tests that appear in this book have been newly compiled, they have not been standardised in comparison to scores obtained by other groups and an actual assessment, for example, an actual IQ measurement, cannot be given. However, there is a guide to assessing your performance at the end of each test, and because many of the tests relate to specific abilities, the results will give you the opportunity to identify your own particular strengths and weaknesses

Psychometric tests broadly fall into two main categories; tests of Maximum performance and tests of Typical performance. Tests of Maximum performance, which include tests of ability and aptitude and include intelligence (IQ) tests, are designed to assess a persons abilities in a specific or general area, whilst tests of Typical performance, such as tests of personality or interest, help build up a profile of an individuals characteristics and personality.

Psychometric tests are being brought more and more into widespread use by employers, mainly because it is important to employers that they place the right people in the right job from the outset. One of the main reasons for this in today's competitive world of tight purse strings, cost cutting and low budgets is the high cost of terminating a poorly made hiring decision.

A position has to be advertised, a short list drawn up from, usually, a large number of applicants, the applicants have to be interviewed and the successful applicant has to be trained. If the wrong person has been selected then the whole expensive, time consuming process has to be repeated.

Additionally there is disruption caused within the organisation, which may have to perform under-strength until the vacant position has been successfully filled.

There can also be serious legal difficulties involved in dispensing with the services of someone who has just been hired, especially if a contract has been signed.

Furthermore, if a new recruit causes personality conflicts within a team or department this may lead to unrest between other members of staff, with the result that the team may under perform.

To prevent the wrong decisions being made, organisations are looking for the right hiring tools, and one of these is psychometric testing.

It is important that different types of tests are evaluated in tandem with each other as it does not necessarily mean that if a person has a particular skill, or has a high measured IQ, that they will be suited to the job. Whilst you may be good at doing something, you may dislike it intensely, and success in most tasks depends on your personal qualities and attitudes.

Section One
Intellectual Ability Tests

Intelligence is the capacity to learn or understand. It is this which determines how efficiently each of us deals with situations as they arise, and how we profit intellectually from our experience.

The tests in this section are designed to give an objective assessment of abilities in a number of disciplines, for example in verbal understanding, numeracy, logic and spatial, or diagrammatic, reasoning skills.

In all tests in this section you should keep strictly to within the time limit otherwise the assessment given will be invalidated.

General Ability Test

An ability test is designed to measure maximum performance and potential in a number of areas. These abilities can be measured separately, or combined to give an assessment of overall general ability. Often tests are constructed so that they relate to a specific job or skill and assess things such as perceptual speed or mechanical reasoning.

Examples of ability tests are; General Intelligence Tests (IQ Tests), knowledge based Attainment Tests, and Aptitude Tests which test the ability to use knowledge.

Ability is a very general term which can be applied to many different types of specific ability. There are, in fact, over fifty different human abilities, although these fall within the following four main categories:

Cognitive reasoning:

verbal, numerical, abstract, perceptual, spatial, mechanical.

A very broad and general definition of the word cognition is; knowing, perceiving, and thinking. It is studied by psychologists because it reveals the extent of a person's ability to think

Psychomotor:

eye, hand coordination

Sensory:

hearing, touch, sense, smell, sight

Physical:

stamina and strength

In the case of most ability tests there is usually:

a set time limit which must be strictly adhered to in order for the test to be valid.

right and wrong answers.

an average score which has been standardised in comparison with a group of people who have taken the same test.

The following test concentrates on overall general ability in the main areas of cognitive reasoning: verbal, numerical and abstract.

Instructions:

A time limit of 80 minutes is allowed.

Calculators may be used to assist with solving numerical questions where preferred.

Question 1

Replace the question marks with the correct words.

A skilled craftsman is   ?   at performing many tasks around the house to great   ?
.

      a. adapt, effect

      b. adapt, affect

      c. adept, effect

      d. adept, affect

Question 2

The third digit is one less than the first digit, the second digit is three more than the third digit, the fourth digit is four less than the first digit and the second digit is two more than the first digit.

What two numbers below are being described above?

        2679   7962   6852

        6582   5714   9672

        5741   8625   4715

Question 3

Which sentence below is most grammatically correct?

a. The ages combined of Peter and Paul are 56 years.

b. The combined age of Peter and Paul are 56 years.

c. The combined ages of Peter and Paul is 56 years.

d. The combined age of Peter and Paul is 56 years.

Question 4

How many identical boxes measuring 1 metre by 1 metre by 50 cm can be packed into a container measuring 7 x 6 x 5 metres?

Question 5

In the course of a 5-day working week a woman spends £3.50 a day on bus fare and £4.75 a day on tube fares.

How much money would she save per week if she bought a weekly combined bus and tube travel pass for £37.75?

Question 6

Replace the question marks with the correct words.

All   ?   those at the very back of the queue gained   ?   to the concert for a nominal   ?   fee.

a. accept, admission, admittance

b. except, admittance, admission

c. accept, admittance, admission

d. except, admission, admittance

Question 7

In a consignment of eggs, 168 were cracked, which was 12 percent of the total number of eggs. How many eggs were in the consignment?

Question 8

Put the instructions below into the correct order.

a. Remove the white pith and leave the fruit quite bare.

b. Add water, then sugar to taste and allow to steep for some time

c. Slice up the fruit and add it to the contents already in the jug

d. Serve chilled

e. Put it into a jug

f. Peel off the rind very thinly

Question 9

Change the position of five words in the sentence below so that it makes complete sense:

During the course of each working day the potential customers handled hundreds of enquiries from centre and customers call.

Question 10

If I drive 200 miles, how many hours will the journey take if I drive at an average speed of 20 mph for 100 miles and an average speed of 40 mph for 100 miles?

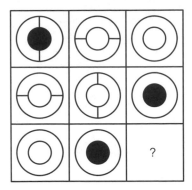

Which is the missing tile?

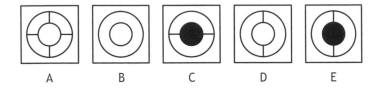

A   B   C   D   E

Jones, Green and Brown supply capital in a new business venture of £30,000, £60,000 and £110,000 respectively. Last year £280,000 profits were available.

How much profit was allocated to each man?

.pdf is to portable document format as .exe is to:

enabled, executable, electronic, extension, encryption.

One millimetre = 0.03937 inches

Therefore, 10 centimetres (one decametre) =   ?   inches

a. 0.3937   b. 3.937   c. 39.37   d. 393.7

Question 15

A photograph measuring 6.4 x 5.5 cm is to be enlarged.

If the enlargement of the longest side is 32 cm, what is the length of the shorter side?

Question 16

A stadium seats 38300 spectators of which 85% are under cover.
How many spectators are not under cover when the stadium is full?

Question 17

Millimetre is to centimetre as centimetre is to decimetre and decimetre is to?

hectometre, metre, kilometre, myrometre, millimetre

Question 18

The combination or connection of states of mind, or their objects, with one another, as a result of which one is said to be revived, or represented, by means of the other.

Which phrase below most closely fits the above definition?

a. learning by trial and error

b. divergent thinking

c. a wild goose chase

d. self-evaluation

e. like-minded

f. spiritual-minded

g. association of ideas

h. wishful thinking

The police decided to   (a)   and let the   (b)   process run its   (c)   knowing that the defendant would have   (d)   to   (e)   at any sentence   (f)   .

From the choices below, fit the correct six words into the sentence.

a. persecute   prosecute

b. judicial   judicious

c. coarse   course

d. recourse   resource

e. appeal   appal

f. passed   past

You have 123 cubic blocks. What is the minimum number that needs to be taken away in order to construct two solid cubes with none left over? Each cube must consist of more than 10 cubic blocks.

Put these four sentences into the correct order.

a. with its help many simple tasks can be performed with maximum efficiency

b. the book contains step-by-step simple instructions

c. as a result, many so-called computer illiterates are fast becoming experts

d. it is lavishly illustrated with numerous diagrams

If five men can build a house in 14 days, how long will it take eight men to build a house assuming all men work at the same rate?

Which of the following sentences is most grammatically correct?

a. it was altogether the strangest of devices despite its imaginative and completely original design

b. it was all together the strangest of devises despite its imaginative and completely original design

c. it was altogether the strangest of devices despite it's imaginative and completely original design

d. it was altogether the strangest of devices despite its imaginary and completely original design

Question 24

A manufacturer produces widgets, but needs to tighten up on the quality control procedures. In a test batch of twenty-five, seven were defective. They then carried out a longer production run in which 648 of 2418 were defective.

Had they improved their quality control performance after the test run?

Question 25

Given that there are 144 square inches in one square foot, and that one square foot is equal to 929.03 square centimetres:

How many square centimetres are there in one square inch?

a. 8.254

b. 6.452

c. 6.258

d. 8.482

e. 8.549

f. 6.386

Question 26

up-date is to revise as default is to: backup, predetermine, edit, erase, input

Question 27

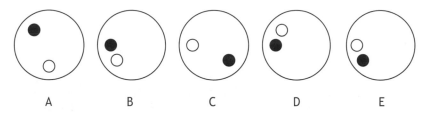

Which circle is missing?

A   B   C   D   E

Question 28

What weight should be placed in the pan in order for the scales to balance?

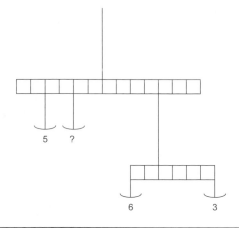

Question 29

throttle is to engine as stopcock is to:

valve, pipe, atrium, water, tighten

The action of forces on bodies at rest.

What branch of mechanics most closely fits the above definition?

      a. inertia

      b. dynamics

      c. statics

      d. kinetics

cube is to six as icosahedron is to:

twelve, sixteen, eighteen, twenty, twenty-four

I went shopping in the market with my sister. At one stall I bought 18 oranges and 12 apples, and my sister bought 6 oranges and 9 apples.
What is the difference between the percentage of oranges to the amount of fruit bought by me and my sister?

Put the following words into alphabetical order:

abetting, Aberdeen, abearing, abessive, Abednego, abeyancy, Aberdare, abetters, aberrate, abettals, abetment, abettors

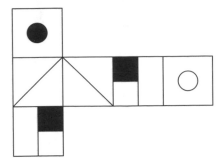

When the above is folded to form a cube, which is the only one of the following that can be produced?

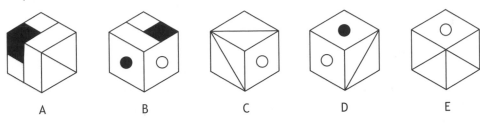

A   B   C   D   E

Which of the following sentences is most grammatically correct?

a. The Gardener's Association took great pride in their allotments, which at this time of the year, always neatly tended, were a pleasure to behold

b. The Gardeners' Association take great pride in their allotments, which at this time of the year, always neatly tended, are a pleasure to behold.

c. The Gardeners' Association took great pride in their allotments, which at this time of the year, always neatly tended, are a pleasure to behold.

d. The Gardener's Association take great pride in their allotments, which at this time of the year, always neatly tended, are a pleasure to behold.

e. The Gardener's Association take great pride in their allotments, which at this time of the year, always neatly tended, were a pleasure to behold.

Question 36

Change the position of four words in the sentence below so that it makes complete sense.

The individual side of the brain reconstructs a whole pattern out of right concepts, at the same time giving rise to new ideas and pieces.

Question 37

A man starts work at 08.30 and ends at 15.45. How many hours does he work in a 6-day working week if he takes 1 hour per day for lunch?

Question 38

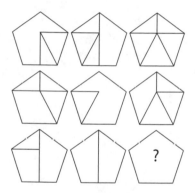

Which pentagon is missing?

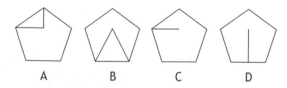

A   B   C   D

Question 39

Change the position of four words in the sentence below so that it makes complete sense.

The essential use of business when writing correct letters is punctuation to convey the writer's exact meaning.

The ages of a group of people are 38, 27, 59, 12, 33, 32, 18, 29, 34 and 68.

What percentage of people in the group is above the average age of the group?

General Intelligence IQ Test

Of all the different methods which purport to measure intelligence, the most famous is the IQ (Intelligence Quotient) test, which is a standardised test designed to measure human intelligence as distinct from attainments.

Intelligence quotient is an age-related measure of intelligence level and is described as 100 times the mental age. The word quotient means the result of dividing one quantity by another, and one definition of intelligence is mental ability or quickness of mind.

Usually, IQ tests consist of a graded series of tasks, each of which has been standardised with a large representative population of individuals in order to establish an average IQ of 100 for each test.

It is generally accepted that a person's mental age remains constant in development to about the age of 13, after which it is shown to slow up, and beyond the age of 18 little or no improvement is found.

When the IQ of a child is measured, the subject attempts an IQ test that has been standardised, with an average score recorded for each age group. Thus a 10-year old child who scored the result that would be expected of a 12-year old would have an IQ of 120, or 12/10 x 100.

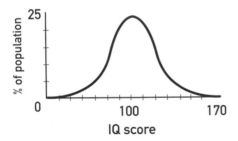

The Bell Curve

Because after the age of 18 little or no improvement is found, adults have to be judged on an IQ test whose average score is 100, and the results graded above and below this norm according to known test scores.

Like so many distributions found in nature, the distribution of IQ takes the form of a fairly regular bell curve in which the average score is 100 and similar proportions occur both above and below this norm.

The following test is very similar in its construction to the General Ability Test on page 5 and concentrates on three main disciplines; verbal ability, numerical ability and spatial reasoning.

Instructions:

A time limit of 80 minutes is allowed.

Calculators may be used to assist with solving numerical questions where preferred.

Question 1

Identify two words (one from each set of brackets) that form a connection (analogy) when paired with the words in capitals.

FOREWORD (book, proceed, write)

OVERTURE (composer, opera, music)

Question 2

9	6	4	6	7
8	7	3	5	4
3	5	9	3	?

What number should replace the question mark?

Question 3

What comes next?

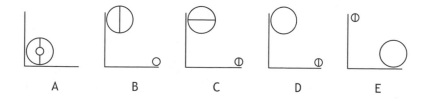

| A | B | C | D | E |

What word in brackets is most opposite to the word in capitals?

RECURRENT (crimson, isolated, prolix, wearisome, stagnated)

Assuming A = 3, B = 4, C = 5, D = 6, E = 7, F = 8
What mathematical sign should replace the question mark?

(A x E) + B = (C x D) ? F + A

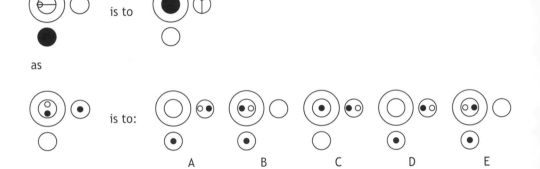

Which word in brackets is closest in meaning to the word in capitals?

INCREASE (mature, renew, augment, efflux, roll).

36	9	85	17
12	2	56	8
48	6	72	8
40	4	55	?

What number should replace the question mark?

Which is the odd one out?

dwelling, building, home, abode, residence

504, 475, ? , 417, 388

What number should replace the question mark?

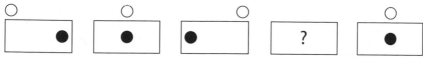

Which is missing?

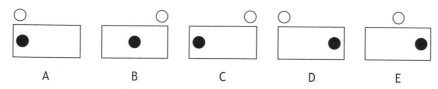

A   B   C   D   E

Which is the odd one out?

tenet, precept, axiom, formula, creed

4936   6848

8756   594?

What number should replace the question mark?

Which word in brackets is closest in meaning to the word in capitals?

STOPGAP (interment, interim, interjection, intern, interface)

What word when placed in the bracket will complete a word or phrase when tacked onto the first word, and start another word or phrase when placed in front of the second word?

third   (.....)   line

Assuming that A = 3, B = 5, C = 7, D = 9 and E = 11, calculate the following.

$$(D - B) \times \frac{(C + E)}{A}$$

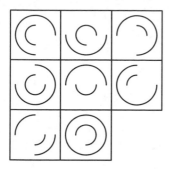

Which is the missing tile?

A   B   C   D   E

Which is the odd one out?

reserved, meditative, reticent, taciturn, uncommunicative

INVENTORY   is to   LIST

as

INDENT   is to: bill, lease, order, document, quantity

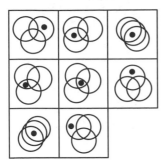

Which is the missing tile?

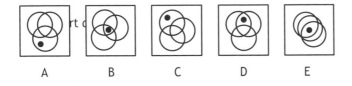

A   B   C   D   E

Sally, Tony and Maria have £78.00 between them. The combined amount of money that Sally and Maria have is twice as much as Tony. The combined amount of money that Tony and Maria have is the same as what Sally has. How much money has each?

Which is the odd one out?

indistinct, impalpable, unapparent, disinclined, hidden

Identify two words (one from each set of brackets) that form a connection (analogy) when paired with the words in capitals.

SPINACH (food, green, vegetable)

SPHAGNUM (grass, moss, fruit)

| 7 | 6 | | 5 | 4 | | 2 | 1 |
| 9 | 5 | | 7 | 3 | | 4 | ? |

What number should replace the question mark?

SNUGLY   (LUNAR)   ARTFUL

In accordance with the rules established above,
what word is coded to appear in the brackets below?

PAELLA   (   )   CHERUB

Which is the odd one out?

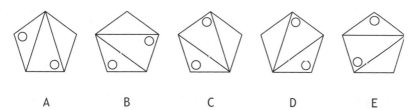

A   B   C   D   E

The most desirable possible under a restriction expressed or implied.

Which word below most closely meets the above definition?

     a. premium

     b. optimum

     c. optimal

     d. premier

Question 28

Which word in brackets is most opposite in meaning to the word in capitals?

MANUMISSION (service, buffoonery, slavery, apathy, stoicism)

Question 29

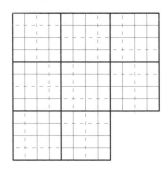

Which is the missing section?

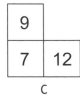

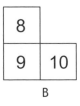

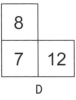

A   B   C   D

Question 30

Which is the missing tile?

  A   B   C   D   E

OWNER   (WISER)   SHINE

In accordance with the rules established above,
what word is coded to appear in the brackets below?

SCORE   (   )   BRAWL

Identify two words (one from each set of brackets) that form a connection
(analogy) when paired with the words in capitals.

PROCLAIM (utter, propound, announce)

ALLEGE (claim, predict, explain)

In five years time the combined age of me and my two daughters will be 99.
What will it be in seven years time?

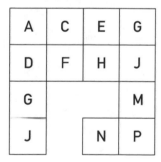

A	C	E	G
D	F	H	J
G			M
J		N	P

Which is the missing section?

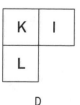

| A | B | C | D |

Question 35

◉ ⊕ ◯   is to

as   (vertical: ◎ ⊕ ●)   is to

◉ ⊕ ◎   ◎ ● ⊕   ⊕ ◎ ●   ⊕ ● ◎   ◎ ⊕ ●
A   B   C   D   E

Question 36

T   Q   N   K   ?

Which letter comes next?

Question 37

Find five consecutive numbers below that total 23.

9735184721896314794

Question 38

BROWSER   is to   VIEW

as

CACHE   is to: **database, store, content, access, search**

Question 39

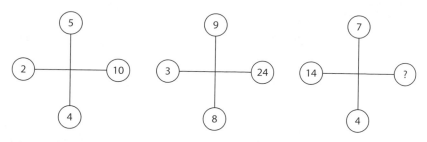

What number should replace the question mark?

Question 40

SYNDICATE   LOGO   DEMURRAGE
DRAWBACK   FLAGSHIP   INCORPORATE
FLOTATION   GOODWILL   LIQUIDATION
MONOPOLY   INTANGIBLE   PARTNERSHIP

From the choice above, match six of the words with the correct definition below.

a. an asset that has a value but no physical existence

b. a companies most impressive or successful product

c. launching a business by means of a share issue

d. exclusive control over a business activity

e. a trademark symbol or emblem

f. form into a registered company

Numerical Aptitude

Numerical questions are widely used in IQ testing and, as numbers are international, numerical tests are regarded as being culture-fair, or culture-free, and designed to be free of any particular cultural bias so that no advantage is derived by individuals of one culture relative to those of another.

These tests, therefore, eliminate language factors or other skills that may be closely tied to another culture, and are frequently designed to test powers of logic, and ability to deal with problems in a structured and analytical way. Individual tests include mental arithmetic, number sequences and logical reasoning, all designed to test a persons aptitude/ability at mathematical calculation, identifying number patterns and the ability to reason with numbers.

Such tests enable employers to test the numerical aptitude of candidates and to determine their proficiency and the extent of their knowledge when dealing with numbers, and their ability to apply this knowledge to the solving of mathematical problems.

Number Sequence Test

In a numerical sequence test it is necessary to identify a pattern that is occurring in the sequence.

The numbers in the sequence may be progressing, or they may be decreasing, and in some cases they may be both progressing and decreasing within the sequence. It is up to you to determine why this is occurring and to either continue the sequence, or to provide a missing number within the sequence.

Example

in the following very simple sequence;

1, 6, 11, ? , 21, 26

Answer

the missing number is 16, as the numbers in the sequence are increasing by 5 each time.

Instructions:

Fill in the missing number/s indicated by the question mark in each question.

A time limit of 20 minutes is allowed.

The use of calculators is not permitted in this test

Question 1

0, 16, 32, ? , 64, 80

Question 2

0, 0, 1, 3, 6, 10, 15, ?

Question 3

1000, 899, 796, 691, 584, 475, ?

Question 4

5, 6, 7, 8, 10, 12, 14, 18, 19, ?

Question 5

3, 4, 2, 5, 1, 6, ?

Question 6

1, 1.5, 3, 7.5, ?

Question 7

100, 93.3, 86.6, 79.9, 73.2, ?

Question 8

10, 100, 13, 97, 19, 91, 28, 79, 40, ?

Question 9

100, 97.5, 92.5, 85, 75, ? , 47.5

Question 10

3, 10, 31, ? , 283, 850

Calculation Test

This test is a battery of ten questions designed to measure your ability to work with numbers and think numerically. It is also a test of your powers of mental arithmetic.

Instructions

A time limit of 30 minutes is allowed.

The use of calculators is not permitted in this test.

Question 1

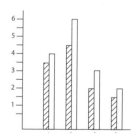

What number is two places away from itself plus 4, three places away from itself less 2, three places away from itself multiplied by 4 and three places away from itself plus 6?

Question 2

Flo is one and a third times as old as Mo, and Mo is one and a third times as old as Joe. Their combined ages are 111. How old are Joe, Mo and Flo?

Question 3

If A = 2, B = 3, C = 4 and D = 5, calculate the following.

$$\frac{(A \times C) + (C \times D)}{(B + C)}$$

Question 4

2873597635962315

Multiply the number of times an even number is immediately followed by an odd number, by the number of times an odd number is immediately followed by an even number, in the list above.

Question 5

How many minutes is it before noon if one hour ago it was three times as many minutes past 8 am?

Question 6

Amy is twice as old as Matthew but two years ago she was four times as old as Matthew. How old is Amy now?

Question 7

What number is a third of fifteen multiplied by 18?

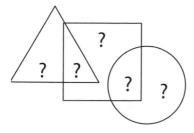

The question marks represent five consecutive numbers.

When added together:

The numbers in the triangle = 37

The numbers in the square = 60

What numbers should replace the question marks?

Insert the numbers 1 - 5 in the circles so that for any particular circle the sum of the numbers in the circles connected directly to it equals the value corresponding to the numbers in that circle as given in the list.

Example

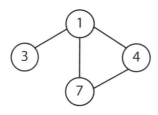

1 = 14 (4 + 7 + 3)

4 = 8 (7 +1)

7 = 5 (4 + 1)

3 = 1

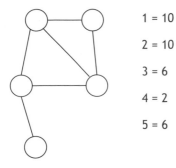

1 = 10

2 = 10

3 = 6

4 = 2

5 = 6

Mary, Tony and Frank have £336.00 between them. The combined amount of money that Mary and Frank have is twice as much as Tony. The combined amount of money that Tony and Frank have is the same as what Mary has.

How much money has each?

Calculation and Logic Test

This test is a battery of ten questions designed to measure your ability to work with numbers and think numerically, and to apply a degree of logical reasoning in order to arrive at the correct answer.

Instructions

A time limit of 45 minutes is allowed.

The use of calculators is permitted in this test

Question 1

What number should replace the question mark?

Question 2

7	9	3	19
4	6	2	12
7	3	8	18
18	18	13	?

What number should replace the question mark?

Question 3

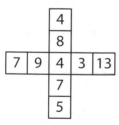 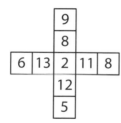 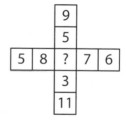

What number should replace the question mark?

Question 4

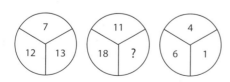

What number should replace the question mark?

	6	
18	39	43
	5	

	15	
12	14	74
	21	

	14	
35	?	36
	7	

What number should replace the question mark?

9	15	18	?
8	19	36	24
7	23	34	11

What number should replace the question mark?

7	4	9	3	2
5	16	6	9	13
22	11	29	18	22
40	51	33	44	40
?	?	?	?	?

What numbers should replace the question marks?

5	4	9	13
6	8	14	22
11	12	23	35
17	20	37	?

What number should replace the question mark?

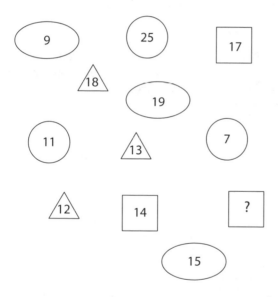

What number should replace the question mark?

What number should replace the question mark?

Numerical Matrix Test

In all ten questions in this test a matrix of numbers is displayed with one section missing. From the four choices presented you have to decide, by looking across each line and by down each column, or at the matrix as a whole, just what pattern of numbers is occurring, and which, therefore, should be the missing section.

Example:

1	2	3	4
5	6	7	8
9			12
13		15	16

Which of the following is the missing section?

11	10
14	

A

14	11
10	

B

10	11
14	

C

10	14
11	

D

Answer:

C: the numbers 1 2 3 4 5 6 7 8 9 10 11 12 13 14 15 16 appear, reading across each row in turn

Instructions

You have 30 minutes in which to complete the ten questions.

The use of a calculator is not permitted in this test, which is designed to test both your mental agility and powers of logical reasoning.

Question 1

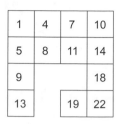

1	4	7	10
5	8	11	14
9			18
13		19	22

Which is the missing section?

11	15
14	

A

12	15
16	

B

11	14
16	

C

12	16
15	

D

Question 2

3	5	7	9
8		14	17
13			25
18	23	28	33

Which is the missing section?

13	
18	20

A

12	
15	23

B

10	
16	24

C

11	
17	21

D

1	2	4	7
		7	10
6		9	12
7	8	10	13

Which is the missing section?

4	5
	7

A

5	6
	7

B

4	5
	8

C

5	6
	8

D

10	14	16	17
11		17	18
13			20
17	21	23	24

Which is the missing section?

15	
16	19

A

16	
17	18

B

15	
17	19

C

16	
18	19

D

4	2	5	5
8	3		6
7			8
9		10	7

Which is the missing section?

	8
6	7
5	

A

	9
5	8
4	

B

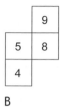

	8
5	8
4	

C

	9
6	7
5	

D

22	19	16	13
		12	9
14		8	5
10			1

Which is the missing section?

17	14	
	10	
	6	3

A

18	15	
	11	
	7	4

B

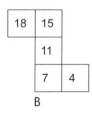

19	16	
	12	
	8	5

C

20	17	
	13	
	9	6

D

5	6	8	9
7	8	10	11
8			
10	11		

Which is the missing section?

10	11	12
	13	14

A

9	10	11
	12	13

B

10	12	13
	14	15

C

9	11	12
	13	14

D

3	8	9	12	15
5	10	15		25
7	14		28	35
2	4		8	10
4			16	20

Which is the missing section?

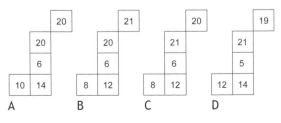

A
	20
20	
6	
10	14

B
	21
20	
6	
8	12

C
	20
21	
6	
8	12

D
	19
21	
5	
12	14

Question 9

1	3	5	7	9
24	21		15	12
28	32	36		44
69	64		54	49
75		87	93	99

Which is the missing section?

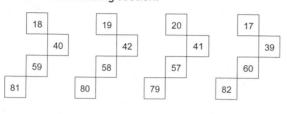

A   B   C   D

Question 10

50	49	48	47	46
56	54	52		48
53			44	41
61		53	49	45
56	51	46	41	36

Which is the missing section?

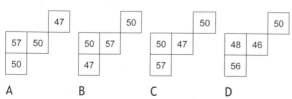

A   B   C   D

Eclectic Numerical Test (calculation and logic)

This test brings together a variety of different types of questions designed to test your ability at mathematical calculation and computation and how well you are able to apply logic when identifying patterns among number series.

Instructions

You have 120 minutes in which to complete the twenty-five questions.

The use of calculators is permitted in this test

Question 1

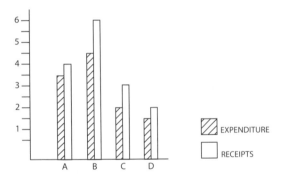

The graph represents four separate enterprises showing expenditure against receipts. Which enterprise showed the highest percentage profit:

A, B, C or D?

Question 2

In the graph shown in question 1, which two enterprises made an identical percentage profit?

0, 100, 7.5, 92.5, 15, 85, 22.5, 77.5, ? , ?

Which two numbers come next?

Question 4

The office received its highest number of emails between 2pm and 3pm,
which was 40% more than the 300 emails it received between 10am and 11am.
On average, how many emails per minute were received between 2pm and 3pm?

Question 5

During the first week of the sale a jacket originally costing £28.00 was reduced by 10%.
At the beginning of the second week the unsold item was marked down by a further 15%.
What was the final sale price?

    a. £22.68

    b. £22.42

    c. £21.68

    d. £21.42

Question 6

If tax is charged at 23% on the first £45,000 and 32% on all income in excess of £45,000,
how much tax is charged on an income of £65,000?

Question 7

100, 99, 97, 94, ? , 85, 79

What number should replace the question mark?

These are the results obtained from two games of Pinball between three players:

Game One:

	Player A	Player B	Player C
Ball 1	126000	98400	1260000
Ball 2	598000	10200	84000
Ball 3	100360	684000	700680

Game Two:

	Player A	Player B	Player C
Ball 1	560000	1500400	48000
Ball 2	290400	680000	795200
Ball 3	700680	102200	900460

Who was the aggregate score overall winner for the two games?

Question 9

Referring again to the table contained in question 8,
which player achieved the lowest three-ball total in game 1,
and which player achieved the highest three-ball total in game 2?

Question 10

Referring again to the table contained in question 8, what, to the nearest 100,
was the average score per ball achieved by the three players over the two games?

If my train journey takes 37 minutes and my taxi journey takes 25 minutes longer, what is my total travelling time in hours and minutes?

In 12 years time the combined age of my four nieces will be 94.
What will it be in five years time?

7469321785917628

Delete all the numbers that appear more than once in the above list and multiply the remaining numbers together. What is the total?

0, 3.6, 7.2, 10.8, 21.6, 25.2, 50.4, ?

What number should replace the question mark?

I started the day with £100.00. In the morning I spent 3/5, in the afternoon I spent 60% of what I had left and in the evening I spent £8.50. How much had I left for my taxi fare home at the end of the day?

Question 16

I completed a journey by bus, rail and taxi. If the train fare cost £56.75, the taxi fare cost £32.85 less than the train and the bus fare cost £21.35 less than the taxi fare, how much did the total journey cost me?

Question 17

1, 1, 2, 3, 4, 5, 8, 7, 16, 9, 32, ?, ?

Which two numbers should replace the question marks?

Question 18

On being surveyed leaving Harrods, 5/16 of women questioned had bought just perfumery, 5/8 had bought just clothing, while the remaining 90 women had just browsed and bought nothing. How many women had bought clothing?

Question 19

39, 78, ? , 156, 195

What number should replace the question mark?

Question 20

What number should replace the question mark?

5	7	10	14
9	11	14	18
12	14	17	
14	16		

Which is the missing section?

A   B   C   D

368	417
627	703
259	286
457	???
198	249

What numbers should replace the question marks?

1, 6, 7, ?, ?, 18, 19, 24, 25

What numbers should replace the question marks?

100, 96.5, 89, 85.5, ?, ?, 67, 63.5

What numbers should replace the question marks?

3124	5306	7568
4205	6427	8??9

What numbers should replace the question marks?

Eclectic Numerical Test (calculation, logic and lateral thinking)

This test brings together a variety of different types of questions designed to test your ability at mathematical calculation and computation and how well you are able to apply logic, and in some cases, a degree of lateral thinking, when identifying patterns among number series.

Instructions

You have 120 minutes in which to complete the twenty-five questions.

The use of calculators is permitted in this test

Question 1

Assuming A = 3, B = 4, C = 5, D = 6; calculate the following:

$$\frac{(A \times D) - A}{C} \quad \times \quad \frac{C - A}{B}$$

Question 2

How many minutes is it before 12 noon if 57 minutes ago it was twice as many minutes past 9am?

Question 3

A statue is being carved by a sculptor. The original piece of marble weighs 250 lbs. In the first month 35% is chipped away, in the second month 20% of the remainder is chipped away and in the third month 25% of the remainder is chipped away, smoothed and polished to produce the final statue.

What is the weight of the final statue?

Question 4

395 : 32

763 : 45

Which numbers below have the same relationship to one another as the numbers above?

        a. 829 : 27

        b. 698 : 62

        c. 358 : 62

        d. 186 : 19

        e. 587 : 20

9547 : 1411 : 52

4896 : 1215 : 36

Which numbers below have the same relationship to one another
as the numbers above?

      a. 5219 : 1020 : 12

      b. 6978 : 1317 : 25

      c. 8274 : 1110 : 22

      d. 5879 : 1318 : 49

      e. 6739 : 1312 : 43

Question 6

      529 (9096) 384

      716 (4240) 542

      393 (?) 429

What number should replace the question mark?

Question 7

      132564 is to 523146

and   798215 is to 289751

therefore   684102 is to ?

Question 8

0.85, 0.85, ?, 5.1, 20.4, 102

What number should replace the question mark?

Question 9

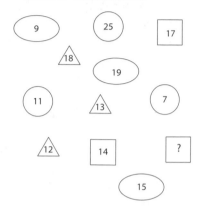

What number should replace the question mark?

Question 10

What is the value of?

$$\left(\frac{297}{594}\right)^2 \times 384$$

Question 11

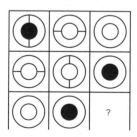

What number should replace the question mark?

Question 12

Place the numbers 1 - 5 in the circles so that:

The sum of the numbers 5 and 3 plus all the numbers between them total 14
The sum of the numbers 2 and 1 plus all the numbers between them total 10
The sum of the numbers 5 and 1 plus all the numbers between them total 15

Question 13

491322

641014

961521

751217

Which number below has the same feature in common with all the numbers above?

a. 281029

b. 581321

c. 791423

d. 981654

e. 391438

Question 14

I have 200 sq. metres of turf with which I intend to cover two rectangular areas of ground, one of which is 15 metres by 11 metres and the other 5.5 by 3.5 metres.

How many sq. metres of turf will I have left over?

A greengrocer ordered 810 items of fruit consisting of a mixture of grapefruit, apples and oranges in the ratio 2 : 3 : 4 respectively.

How many of each fruit did he order?

29, 92, 32, 89, 38, 83, 50, 71, 74, ?

What number should replace the question mark?

Tins of peas cost 3 pence (£0.03) more if bought individually than if bought in packs of 8. If a pack of 8 costs £2.48, what is the cost of five tins?

A train ticket costs £25.00 before 9.30am and £21.25 after 9.30am. What percentage saving does this represent for people travelling after 9.30am?

4	6	3	2	1
10	7	8	4	3
17	18	11	11	7
35	28	29	18	18
63	?	?	?	36

What numbers should replace the question marks?

Question 20

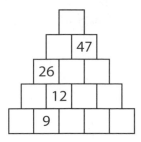

Complete the pyramid so that each number in the pyramid is the sum of the two numbers directly below it.

Question 21

Out of 240 guests at a conference, a quarter took their coffee with both milk and sugar, 3/8 took it with just milk, 3/16 took it with sugar only and the rest took it black with neither milk nor sugar.

How many guests took it with neither milk nor sugar?

Question 22

What number should replace the question mark?

Question 23

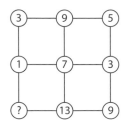

What number should replace the question mark?

Question 24

3	4	9
2	8	4

6	9	8
5	6	?

What number should replace the question mark?

Question 25

6	5	4	2	7	1
5	3	6	4	7	2
2	8	3	5	6	7
3	8	5	7	4	6
8	7	6	4	9	3
7	5	8	6	9	?

What number should replace the question mark?

Verbal Aptitude

Mastery of words is seen by many as having in one's possession the ability to produce order out of chaos and it is argued, therefore, that command of vocabulary is a true measure of intelligence.

Verbal reasoning tests are designed to measure basic verbal ability (the ability to understand and use words), and typically include spelling, grammar, word meanings, completing sentences, synonyms and antonyms.

Classification Test

In this test you are given a list of five words and are required to choose which of the five words is the odd one out. This may be for a variety of reasons.

Example:

a. calm, quiet, relaxed, serene, unruffled

Quiet is the odd one out as the rest mean the same thing. However, your being quiet does not necessarily mean that you are calm, relaxed serene or unruffled. You could be extremely upset and agitated but still remain quiet.

Example 2:

b. abode, dwelling, house, residence, street

Street is the odd one out as the rest are specific places in which we live. Street is a general term which may contain many houses, gardens, trees, road surfaces etc.

We all have the ability to classify objects into groups. We all know, for example, that beech, elm, oak and willow are types of trees, so that if we suddenly introduce daffodil into the list, it will then be the odd one out because it is a flower. This type of thinking is that which is required to solve the questions in this test, and also called for is flexibility of thought, in view of the different reasons why one item is the odd one out.

In order to solve such questions one strategy which may be adopted is to first consider what all the other items have in common, for example, before deciding which one of a group is the odd one out you must decide what feature or condition is possessed by four of the group that is not shared by the fifth.

Instructions:

In each of the following select one word from the choice of five words provided which is the odd one out.

You have 10 minutes in which to solve the ten questions.

Question 1

spectral, ghostly, demonic, wraithlike, phantasmal

Question 2

erudite, cultured, highbrow, intellectual, guileful

Question 3

resolute, independent, steadfast, dogged, purposeful

Question 4

dissimulating, unemotional, insensitive, indolent, indifferent

Question 5

chair, bench, throne, ladder, stool

Question 6

conceivable, imaginable, plausible, polemic, credible

Question 7

abundance, quantity, plethora, profusion, multitude

Question 8

prairie, savannah, campo, sierra, pampas

Question 9

verso, sinistral, larboard, dextral, southpaw

Question 10

witter, simper, rabbit, prate, maunder

Synonym Test

A synonym is a word having the same, or very similar, meaning to another of the same language. Examples of synonyms are: select and choose, easy and elementary, inquire and probe.

This test is a series of ten questions designed to test your knowledge of language and your ability to quickly identify words that have the same or very similar meanings.

Instructions:

You have 10 minutes in which to solve the ten questions.

You should read the instructions to each question, or set of questions carefully.

Questions 1 - 5
In questions 1 – 5 select one word in the brackets that is closest in meaning to the word in capitals.

Question 1

HIATUS (injunction, abatement, hybrid, retreat, merriment)

Question 2

EARMARK (cover, arrange, select, assign, manage)

Question 3

ONEROUS (ocular, taxing, menacing, harassing, poor)

CORNUCOPIA (warmth, density, profusion, fecundity, instrument)

ABTRUSE (recondite, embarrass, temporary, alongside, scornful)

Which word below means belonging or relating to winter?

    a. supernal

    b. hibernal

    c. asternal

    d. sempiternal

    e. sternal

Which word below means the right to vote?

    a. selvage

    b. courage

    c. saxifrage

    d. arbitrage

    e. suffrage

Questions 8 - 10

In each of questions 8 – 10 select the two words which are closest in meaning.

Question 8

rejection, cancellation, criticism, abrogation, backlash, subjugation

Question 9

covet, envision, propound, charm, anticipate, enshroud

Question 10

wry, improper, sullen, blasé, askew, insolent

Antonym Test

An antonym is a word with the opposite meaning to another of the same language. Examples of antonyms are big and small, true and false, happy and sad.

This test is a series of ten questions designed to test your knowledge of language and your ability to quickly identify words that are most opposite in meaning.

Instructions:

You have 10 minutes in which to solve the ten questions.

You should read the instructions to each question, or set of questions carefully.

Questions 1 - 5

In questions 1 – 5 select one word in the brackets that is most opposite in meaning to the word in capitals.

Question 1

FRIVOLOUS (moody, cynical, regal, solemn, prolix)

ENTHUSIASTIC (vehement, reluctant, extraneous, transient, irregular)

Question 3

GLUT (emaciate, narrow, capacity, heavy, paucity)

Question 4

DETENTION (hope, liberation, peace, espousal, authorisation)

Question 5

MITIGATE (heighten, straighten, lengthen, chasten, embolden)

Questions 6 - 10
In each of questions 6 - 10 select the two words that are most opposite in meaning.

Question 6

artistic, pastel, masterful, vibrant, idyllic, active

Question 7

impractical, real, fluent, feigned, absurd, immoral

Question 8

withdrawn, proficient, piquant, wretched, accessible, acclaimed

Question 9

adjacent, straight, remote, identical, forsaken, recent

council, venture, asset, facet, encumbrance, trick

Analogy Test

An analogy is a similitude of relations where it is necessary to reason the answer from a parallel case.

In an analogies test the testee is required to complete an analogous relationship.

Questions may take the form A is to B as C is to?

Example:

HELMET is to protection as TIARA is to adornment,
queen, hair, royalty, head

The answer is adornment. Both a helmet and a tiara are worn on the head, however, a helmet is worn for the purpose of protection and a tiara is worn for adornment.

Instructions

You have 15 minutes in which to solve the ten questions.

You should read the instructions to each question, or set of questions carefully.

Questions 1 - 6
Identify two words (one from each set of brackets) that form a connection (analogy) when paired with the words in capitals.

Question 1

MATERNAL (aunt, parent, mother)

FRATERNAL (brother, father, sister)

Question 2

ASTERISK (dash, bracket, star)

OBELISK (bullet, dagger, slash)

Question 3

KILO- (hundred, thousand, million)

MILLI- (thousandth, millionth, hundredth)

Question 4

CISTERN (water, tank, hydrant)

AQUADUCT (pipe, estuary, canal)

Question 5

PRECEDENCE (priority, example, order)

PRECEDENTS (examples, orders, priorities)

Question 6

LANDLORD (lesser, lessor, lessee)

TENANT (lessee, lessor, lesser)

Questions 7 - 10
In each question, select one word from the five options given
to correctly complete the analogy.

Question 7

SCALENE   is to   TRIANGLE

as

RHOMBUS   is to: shape, quadrilateral, square, equilateral, trapezium

Question 8

LINEAR MEASURE   is to   LENGTH

as

LIQUID MEASURE   is to: **gallon, capacity, volume, density, fluidity**

Question 9

CHISEL   is to   CHIP

as

RASP   is to: **cut, file, chop, gouge, hew**

Question 10

CUPROUS   is to   COPPER

as

FERROUS   is to: **zinc, lead, iron, tin, metal**

Eclectic Verbal Ability Test 1

This test is a miscellaneous selection of twenty-five verbal questions designed to measure language use or comprehension and your ability to adapt to different types of question.

Instructions:

You have 90 minutes in which to solve the twenty-five questions.

You should read the instructions to each question carefully.

The combination of learning and ··· is the ··· of all our ··· and abilities and is what ··· us to ··· the past, ··· in the ··· and ··· for the ··· .

Place the missing nine words below correctly into the above passage.

exist	plan	knowledge
consider	enables	future
basis	present	memory

There was broad agreement in ··· as to which of the two main proposals should take immediate ··· .

Which pair of words below is missing from the above sentence?

a. principle, affect

b. principal, affect

c. principle, effect

d. principal, effect

Bees ··· their ··· in ··· that are ··· with ··· shapes, simply because ··· fit ··· with no loss of ··· .

Fill in the missing eight words below correctly into the above passage.

hexagon	honey	together	filled
space	hexagons	manufacture	hives

Which of the following is the most accurate definition of the word FALLACY?

a. illogical reasoning or argument that is knowingly invalid and deliberately misleading

b. illogical or irrelevant conclusion or statement

c. illogical reasoning or faulty argument that invalidates the conclusion

d. illogical reasoning or argument, though not deliberately so

Question 5

Which one of the following sentences is most grammatically correct?

a. The brother-in-laws of the brides cousins' lined up for the photographer.

b. The brothers-in-law of the brides cousin's lined up for the photographer

c. The brother-in-laws of the bride's cousins lined up for the photographer

d. The brothers-in-law of the bride's cousins lined up for the photographer.

e. The brother's-in-law of the bride's cousins lined up for the photographer.

Question 6

Identify two words (one from each set of brackets) that form a connection (analogy) when paired with the words in capitals.

WHERE (question, never, Paris)

WHEN (soon, train, time)

Identify two words (one from each set of brackets) that form a connection (analogy) when paired with the words in capitals.

CONCEPT (method, notion, whim)

FIXATION (premise, idea, preconception)

BKR   is to   EHU

as

NSV   is to: KPS, PQX, QPY, ROZ, LUT

A	B	D
G	K	?

What letter is missing?

A	B	C	?
C	E	G	?
E	H	K	?

Which letters are missing from the end column?

Identify two words (one from each set of brackets) that form a connection (analogy) when paired with the words in capitals.

CIRCLE (length, diameter, area)

TRIANGLE (height, radius, hypotenuse)

Which two words are closest in meaning?

abusive, arcane, punitive, caustic, vindictive, paltry

Which two words are most opposite in meaning?

liberal, mundane, dulcet, fresh, interesting, furtive

Which one of the sentences below is most grammatically correct?

a. As the procession made it's way down the Mall, one spectator remarked, "I have been here on three separate occasions but it's the first time the sun has shined so brightly".

b. As the procession made its way down the Mall, one spectator remarked, "I have been here on three seperate occasions but it's the first time the sun has shined so brightly".

c. As the procession made its way down the Mall, one spectator remarked, "I have been here on three separate occasions but it's the first time the sun has shined so brightly".

d. As the procession made it's way down the Mall, one spectator remarked, "I have been here on three separate occasions but it's the first time the sun shone so brightly".

e. As the procession made it's way down the Mall, one spectator remarked, "I have been here on three seperate occasions but it's the first time the sun has shined so brightly".

All antique artefacts that are genuine artefacts are antiques.

Therefore:

To be antiques, artefacts must be genuine.

Is that:

      a. true

      b. false

      c. not possible to say

Question 16

CIRCUMSPECT is to GUARDED as POLITIC is to careful, discreet, electable, reserved, expedient

Question 17

The stock market crash had   ***   consequences for the   *** .

Which pair of words below is missing from the above sentence?

      a. disastrous, investers

      b. disasterous, investors

      c. disastrous, investors

      d. disasterous, investers

Question 18

Which two words are most opposite in meaning?

      migrate, expand, unravel, wane, exculpate, assay

On passing judgement his worship took great care to   ***   the right   ***.

Which pair of words below is missing from the above sentence?

       a. cite, precedence

       b. sight, precedence

       c. site, precedents

       d. cite, precedents

       e. sight, precedents

       f. site, precedence

Question 20

Which word in brackets means the same as the word in capitals?

       GREGARIOUS (reserved, hungry, generous, affable, ferocious)

Question 21

Which word in brackets is opposite in meaning to the word in capitals?

       PIQUANT (slow, tart, pleased, bland, irreverent)

Question 22

Which is the odd one out?

       surpass, outstrip, exceed, outwit, surmount

Question 23

       AB, ABD, ABDG, ABDGK, ?

What comes next?

Which four bits can be joined together to form two words that have the same meanings?

ton, ase, pel, end, car, pro, esc, nch, ple, int, lau, ort

Which four-letter word means the same as the definitions either side of the brackets?

upright and respectable (**) by a small margin**

Eclectic Verbal Ability Test 2

This test is a miscellaneous selection of twenty-five verbal questions designed to measure language use or comprehension and your ability to adapt to different types of question, and in a number of instances apply a degree of logical analysis in order to arrive at the correct answer.

Instructions:

You have 90 minutes in which to solve the twenty-five questions.

You should read the instructions to each question carefully.

Question 1

obtuse, tureen, reader, ?

What word, logically, continues the above sequence?

> a. damage
>
> b. adhere
>
> c. depart
>
> d. indict
>
> e. prefer

What is the meaning of extemporaneously?

      a. not within set limits

      b. in a disingenuous manner

      c. in an articulate manner

      d. without prior preparation

      e. beyond belief

Question 3

RANKLE   (EUREKA)   SALUTE

What word is coded to appear in the brackets below, in accordance with the rules established above?

FOREST   (******)   UNIONS

Question 4

Which word below is a synonym of the phrase; fan the flames of?

      a. enhance

      b. exacerbate

      c. confabulate

      d. exasperate

      e. brighten

Question 5

STAY is to REMAIN as PEREGRINATE is to: linger, travel, abscond, disappear, discard

Question 6

Which two phrases are closest in meaning?

    a. lack of zeal

    b. lack of forethought

    c. lack of inhibition

    d. lack of charm

    e. lack of restraint

Question 7

```
    *    E    N

    E    *    D

    L    R    A
```

Start at one of the four corner letters and spiral clockwise round the perimeter, finishing at the centre letter to spell out a nine-letter word. You must provide the missing letters.

Question 8

Change one letter only in each of the words below to produce a familiar phrase.

AND TILE ROW

Question 9

Use every letter of the newspaper headline below once each only to spell out three shades of brown.

NUT HUNT LAZES A CHERUB

Question 10

Only one group of six letters below can be arranged to spell out a six-letter word in the English language. What is the word?

ILOYSN

YACOLE

EKOPDA

ROANEY

Question 11

Which of the following is not an anagram of a country beginning with the letter B?

a. bad boars

b. ban hut

c. baa lain

d. ural gabi

Question 12

Find two words, one in each circle, both reading clockwise that are synonyms. You must provide the missing letters.

L	I	E		
T	S	A		
C	P	C	I	V
	E	O	C	
	N	D	N	

Each square contains the letters of two nine-letter words
that are opposite in meaning. Find the two words.

Which two words are closest in meaning?

district, assembly, consortium, anthology, category, conglomerate

GRAPHICS   is to   DRAWING

as

SEMANTICS   is to: style, language, ethics, writing, location

HE ADHERES LOVE is an anagram of which familiar phrase (4, 4, 5 letters long)

Clue: topsy-turvy

What four-letter word completes the word on the left and starts the word on the right?

under ···· age

Question 18

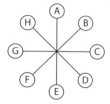

What letter is two letters clockwise from the letter directly opposite the letter three letters anti-clockwise from the letter D?

Question 19

Find two words, one in each circle, both reading clockwise that are antonyms. You must provide the missing letters.

Question 20

What do the following words all have in common?

event, trigger, medium, landing, slap

Question 21

Put the following eight words in alphabetical order.

acetarious, acervative, acetonemia, acephalist, acetimeter, acervuline, acetometer, acerbitude

Question 22

Which two words are closest in meaning?

paragon, allegory, archetype, limit, spectacle, stalwart

javelin, jocular, lexicon, ?

What, logically, comes next?

      a. tutored

      b. sugared

      c. demonic

      d. dowager

      e. liberal

The quality or state of being transparent or translucent.

Which word below does not fit the above definition?

      a. clear

      b. lucidity

      c. rationality

      d. directness

      e. perspicuity

What, logically, should be the missing word?

      true (protrude) drop

      ? (overhang) horn

Spatial Aptitude

The definition of spatial is pertaining to space, and spatial abilities mean the perceptual and cognitive abilities that enable a person to deal with spatial relations.

This type of abstract reasoning does not involve problems that are verbal or numerical in nature. The questions within such tests usually take the form of a series of shapes or diagrams from which you have to pick the odd one out, or identify which should come next in a sequence from a set of alternatives, or choose from a set of alternatives which diagram will complete an analogy. The ability being investigated in this type of test is how well a person is able to identify patterns and meaning from what might appear at first glance random or very complex information.

Whilst such tests of spatial aptitude set out to measure general intellectual reasoning, they are designed not just to test your powers of logic and your ability to deal with problems in a structured and analytical way, but also to make you think laterally and creatively.

Whilst mastery of words is seen by many as the true measure of intelligence, there is a belief that diagrammatic tests of spatial aptitude and abstract reasoning are more important as they examine raw intelligence without the influence of prior knowledge.

Such tests are referred to as culture-free or culture-fair tests, and are designed to be free of any cultural bias, so that no advantage is derived by individuals of one culture relative to those of another. In other words, they eliminate language factors or other skills that might be closely tied to one particular culture.

Visual Odd One Out Test

This test consists of a series of ten questions in which you are presented with a set of shapes or diagrams from which you have to choose the odd one out.

Instructions

A time limit of 20 minutes is allowed.

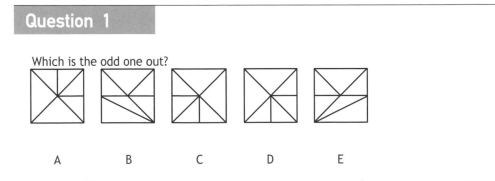

Which is the odd one out?

A   B   C   D   E

Question 2

Which is the odd one out?

A   B   C   D   E

Question 3

Which is the odd one out?

A   B   C   D   E

Question 4

Which is the odd one out?

A   B   C   D   E

Question 5

Which is the odd one out?

A   B   C   D   E

Question 6

Which is the odd one out?

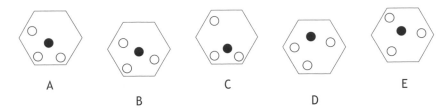

A   B   C   D   E

Question 7

Which is the odd one out?

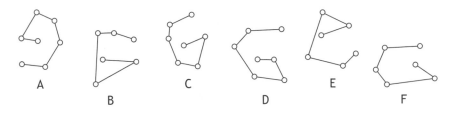

A   B   C   D   E   F

Question 8

Which is the odd one out?

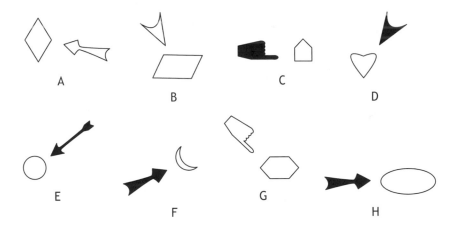

A   B   C   D   E   F   G   H

Which is the odd one out?

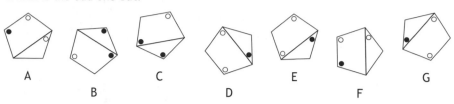

A   B   C   D   E   F   G

Question 10

Which is the odd one out?

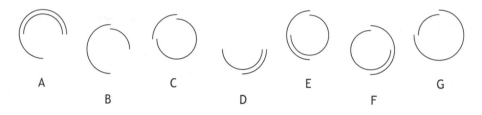

A   B   C   D   E   F   G

Visual Sequence Test

This test consists of a series of ten questions in which you are presented with a set of shapes or diagrams which form a logical sequence, and from the information provided you have to choose from the set of alternatives provided, what comes next in the sequence.

Instructions

A time limit of 20 minutes is allowed.

Question 1

What comes next?

A   B   C   D   E

Question 2

What comes next?

A   B   C   D   E

Question 3

What comes next?

A   B   C   D   E

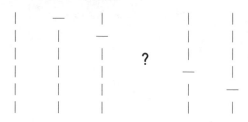

Which is missing?

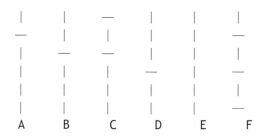

A   B   C   D   E   F

What comes next?

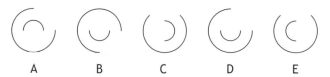

A   B   C   D   E

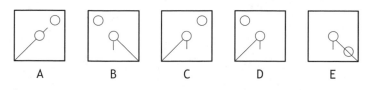

What comes next?

A   B   C   D   E

Question 7

Which is missing?

| A | B | C | D | E |

Question 8

What comes next?

| A | B | C | D | E |

Question 9

Which is missing?

| A | B | C | D | E |

?

What comes next?

| A | B | C | D | E |

Visual Analogy Test:

As in the case of the verbal analogy test on page ..., in each of the ten questions in this test it is necessary to reason the answer from a parallel case. In each question you are required to choose, from a set of alternatives, which diagram will complete a similar analogy to the first example.

Instructions

A time limit of 20 minutes is allowed.

Question 1

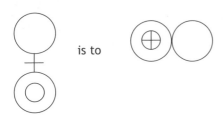

is to

as

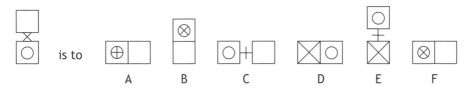

is to   A   B   C   D   E   F

Question 2

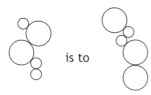

is to

as

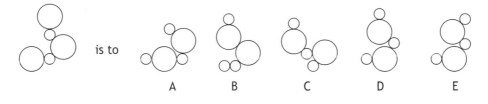

is to   A   B   C   D   E

Question 3

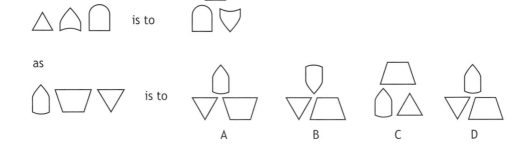

is to

as

is to   A   B   C   D

Question 4

  is to

as

 is to

A   B   C   D

Question 5

 is to

as

 is to

A   B   C   D   E

Question 6

 is to

as

 is to    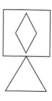

A   B   C   D   E

Question 7

  is to

as

  is to

                                          A   B   C   D   E

Question 8

  is to

as

  is to

                                       A   B   C   D   E

Question 9

  is to   (see above)

as

  is to

                          A   B   C   D   E   F

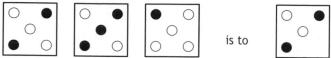 is to

as

   is to

  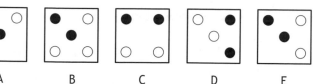

A   B   C   D   E

Technical Aptitude

Technical aptitude assessment is becoming increasingly more prevalent as part of an employer's selection procedure. Employees with a higher scientific and technical aptitude have the potential to master technology much more effectively than candidates with a lower technical aptitude. Employing them in technology oriented jobs is, therefore, considerably more cost-effective, in terms of both training and efficiency of performance in carrying out the job at the desired level.

A candidate who scores highly on a technical aptitude test has, therefore, a higher potential for achievement in a technological business environment, and this requirement is particularly important, for example, with the explosion of information technology. As new technology continues to emerge and develop, it is important to employers that they have the means at their disposal to identify candidates who are able to learn these new technologies quickly and be able to apply these skills in order to solve complex problems in their jobs.

The following test consists of fifteen questions which are designed to test your general scientific knowledge, technical aptitude and powers of mechanical reasoning and logic.

Instructions:

A time limit of 60 minutes is allowed.

The use of calculators is permitted in this test

Question 1

Put a tick against which two of these statements you believe to be correct:

a. A gear with 10 teeth driving a gear with 20 teeth will revolve twice as fast as the gear it is driving

b. A gear with 10 teeth driving a gear with 20 teeth will revolve half as fast as the gear it is driving

c. A 20-tooth gear driving a 10-tooth gear will revolve at twice the speed as the gear it is driving

d. A 20-tooth gear driving a 10-tooth gear will revolve at half the speed of the gear it is driving.

Question 2

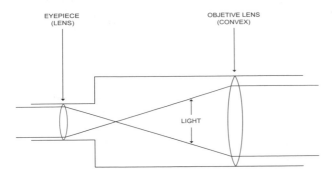

EYEPIECE
(LENS)

OBJETIVE LENS
(CONVEX)

LIGHT

The above is a cross-section of a simple version of which device?

Question 3

*** is the ratio of the mass of a body to its volume.

Fill in the missing word or words:

        a. space

        b. weight

        c. density

        d. power

        e. gravity

        f. kinetic energy

Question 4

The investigation of human, physical and mental abilities and the application of this knowledge in products, equipment and artificial environments.

Which word below most closely meets the above definition?

    a. ethics

    b. ergonomics

    c. mechanics

    d. logistics

    e. eugenics

Question 5

Which part of the wheelbarrow is the fulcrum?

Question 6

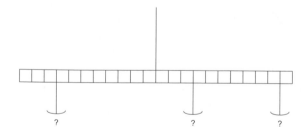

Insert the three weights 4g, 6g and 9g, one into each of the three pans, so that the scales balance perfectly.

Some Mopalops are two-footed
All Flopalops are Mopalops
Therefore, all Flopalops are two-footed.

Is the conclusion:

a. true

b. false

c. not proven

cruciform   is to   **cross**

as   **cuneiform**   is to: claw, wedge, bell, rectangle, star.

A four-sided figure in which the two pairs of opposite sides only are of equal length and opposite angles are equal, but not 90°.

What figure is being described above?

a. rectangle

b. rhombus

c. parallelogram

d. trapezium

e. kite

Question 10

In the Binary system the number 0 is represented as 0000 and the number 15 as 1111.

In accordance with the rules established in the table below, how, in Binary, is the number 10 represented?

	8	4	2	1
0	0	0	0	0
1	0	0	0	1
2	0	0	1	0
3	0	0	1	1
4	0	1	0	0
5	0	1	0	1
6	0	1	1	0
7	0	1	1	1
8	1	0	0	0
9	1	0	0	1
10	?	?	?	?
11	1	0	1	1
12	1	1	0	0
13	1	1	0	1
14	1	1	1	0
15	1	1	1	1

Fill in the missing number:

$$175 - 13 = 143 + ?$$

Which mathematical sign is missing?

$$65 \ ? \ 0.2 = 260 + 65$$

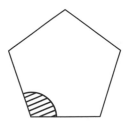

What is the value of the shaded angle?

Given that 10 millimetres (mm) = 1 centimetre (cm)
and 100 cm = 1 metre (m)

What figure in cm is missing from the equation?

$$? + 200cm + 72mm = 3.6m$$

The elephant exerts a force of 50,000 Newtons on the plank
and the girl exerts a force of just 250 Newtons on the plank
How far does the girl need to walk along the plank
in order to balance the elephant?

Advanced Intelligence (IQ) Test

This test consists of a battery of 40 questions designed to test a slightly higher level of verbal, numerical and spatial ability and reasoning/ problem solving capabilities than the test on page number 19.

Instructions:

A time limit of 120 minutes is allowed.

Calculators may be used to assist with solving numerical questions where preferred.

Question 1

Which two words are closest in meaning?

delightful, platitudinous, credible, hackneyed, artificial, gratifying

Question 2

Which two words are closest in meaning?

reliable, mercurial, humane, changeable, admirable, symbolic

Question 3

That which affords convenience, advantage or profit, especially in commerce including goods, wares, merchandise, produce of land and manufacture.

What word below most closely fits the above definition?

a. inventory

b. commodity

c. assets

d. security

e. turnover

Which two words are most opposite in meaning?

beneficial, sentient, noxious, overt, inoffensive, copious

Question 5

Which two words are most opposite in meaning?

flawed, evident, erect, recumbent, meteoric, erudite

Question 6

popularity is to acclaim as popularly is to:

crowded, generally, occupied, favoured, famous, dominant

Question 7

improvised is to unrehearsed as unprompted is to:

spontaneous, fortuitous, unexpected, unpremeditated, unchallenged

Question 8

Identify two words (one from each set of brackets) that form a connection (analogy) when paired with the words in capitals.

JUDGEMENT (affidavit, decision, committal)

INJUNCTION (deed, order, document)

Question 9

Identify two words (one from each set of brackets) that form a connection (analogy) when paired with the words in capitals.

DIVIDEND (option, liability, distribution)

EQUITY (assets, bond, investments)

Which two words are opposite in meaning?

value, discount, debt, bonus, premium, portfolio

A B   M N   S T

E D   Q P   ? ?

Which two letters should replace the question marks?

NIMBLER TWEED is an anagram of what 12-letter word, meaning tangle or confusion, which is missing from the sentence below?

He soon lost all traces of it amid a ------------ of tree trunks and underbrush.

Only one group of 5 letters below can be re-arranged to spell out a 5-letter word in the English language. Identify the word.

MEBIL

RIOPC

LETOC

UDFON

HENTU

Question 14

Which words, one from each set of brackets, will correctly complete the sentence?

The **(eminent, imminent)** professor, **(whose, who's)** **(momentous, momentary)** work on neurobiological research had won him widespread acclaim, was **(complemented, complimented)** by the students, who at the end of his lecture rewarded him by a full ten minutes **(continuous, continual)** ovation.

Question 15

A   B   C   D   E   F   G   H

What letter is three letters to the right of the letter which is immediately to the left of the letter, which comes midway between the letters A and G?

Question 16

What word can be placed in front of all the words below to produce, in each case, a familiar word or phrase?

entry, standard, check, space

Question 17

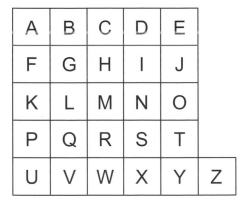

Which letter is two letters below the letter which is immediately to the left of the letter, three letters above the letter which is two letters to the left of the letter Z?

Question 18

Which is the odd one out?

sanctum, university, refectory, vestibule, dispensary

Question 19

Which is the odd one out?

spiral, volute, orb, helix, whorl

Question 20

5	4	9	13
7	8	15	23
12			36
19	20		59

Which is the missing section?

14	26
	41

A

12	24
	41

B

12	24
	39

C

14	26
	39

D

2	4	6	8	10
5				13
8	10		14	16
11	13			19
14	16		20	22

Which is the missing section?

A

6	9	12
	12	
	15	17
	19	

B

7	8	10
	11	
	15	18
	18	

C

6	8	11
	11	
	16	18
	19	

D

7	9	11
	12	
	15	17
	18	

Question 22

100, 96.4, 92.8, 89.2, 85.6, ? ,78.4

What number should replace the question mark?

Question 23

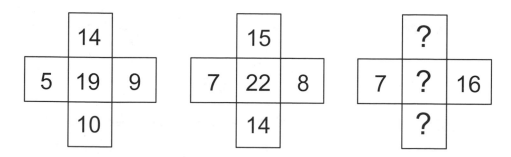

What numbers should replace the question marks?

Question 24

How many minutes is it before 12 noon if in four minutes time it will be three times as many minutes past 11 am?

Question 25

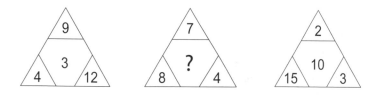

What number should replace the question mark?

Mary has four times as many as Sally and Sally has three times as many as Tony.
Altogether they have 64. How many has Sally?

Question 27

7438	(1822)	9216
3976	(1816)	2192
7569	(12 - -)	8743

What numbers are missing from the third bracket?

Question 28

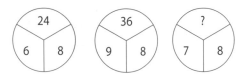

What number should replace the question mark?

Question 29

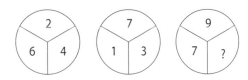

What number should replace the question mark?

1	2	3	4
2	3	4	1
4	1		
3	4		2

Which is the missing section?

2	1
3	

A

2	4
1	

B

2	3
1	

C

2	4
3	

D

8	2	4	4
4	12	3	16
6	4	8	3
9	2	6	?

What number should replace the question mark?

Question 32

I set two clocks at midnight. It later transpired that one of the clocks went, on average, two minutes per hour too slow, and the other went, on average, three minutes per hour too fast, as when I looked at them later that same day, the faster one was exactly one hour ahead of the other.

What was the correct time when I looked at the clocks?

Question 33

Which is missing?

A   B   C   D   E

Question 34

Which is the odd one out?

A   B   C   D   E

Question 35

as

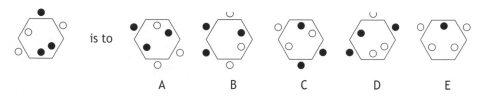

A   B   C   D   E

Question 36

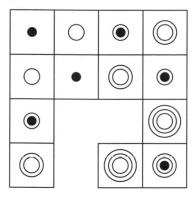

Which is the missing section?

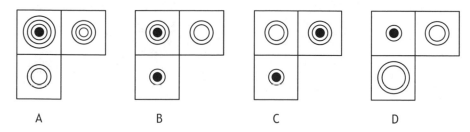

A   B   C   D

Question 37

To which two hexagons below can a dot be added so that they then meet the same conditions as in the hexagon above?

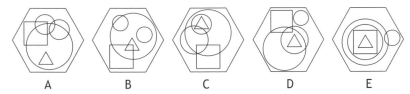

Question 38

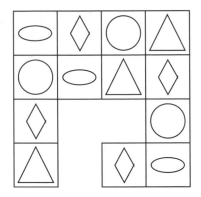

Which is the missing section?

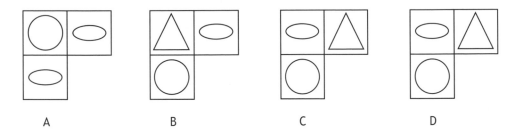

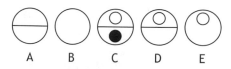

Which is missing?

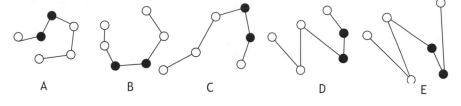

A   B   C   D   E

Which is the odd one out?

A   B   C   D   E

Section Two
Personality Testing

Aptitude testing is just one part of the interview or selection process. Although scoring highly in an aptitude test may impress a prospective employer, it does not reveal the full story as it does not automatically follow that the applicant will be suited to the position for which they are applying. Whilst they may be well suited and qualified to do the actual job, it may be that they do not actually enjoy many aspects of the work involved, which will mean that they would very likely under perform.

To prevent such a mismatch occurring it is likely that when attending an interview you would be asked to participate in a personality profiling test. Such a test would measure personality traits, for example, how you relate to other people; how you relate to emotions, both your own and your colleagues; how you respond to stressful situations; or what motivates you.

In general, the term personality refers to the patterns of thought, feeling and behaviour that are unique in every one of us, and these are the characteristics that distinguish us from other people. Our personality thus implies the predictability of how we are likely to act or react under different circumstances, although in reality nothing is quite that simple and our reactions to situations are never so predictable.

Although personality questionnaires are usually described as tests, this can be misleading since they do not have pass or fail scores, nor are they usually timed.

In the case of personality tests, there is sometimes a temptation for young interviewees, so used to tests at University, to try and beat the test by determining what the correct answer should be, however, it is important that whenever you are faced with a personality questionnaire you answer each question honestly.

Any attempt to guess the correct answer, in other words the answer you think your pro-spective employer wants to hear, has every chance of being noticed when your results are analysed or when the face-to-face interview takes place. Also tests often guard against such manipulation by posing the same question more than once, but in a different way.

At all times, therefore, candidates should simply follow the instructions and be honest with the answers. In the unlikely event of candidates beating the test, then they have not done themselves any favours as this could result in them being offered a job that does not suit them, and this could be an unfortunate and unhappy start to their career.

The following three tests are typical of the type of test that candidates may be asked to complete. They are designed to explore your personality in three key areas, that of ambition to succeed, self-confidence and leadership qualities. The tests are also designed to make you think about your own aspirations, and to help you to maximise your performance in the areas under examination.

Instructions:

In each of the three tests, for each question or statement choose from a scale of 1 - 5 which of these statements you most agree with or is most applicable to yourself. Choose just one of the numbers 1 - 5 in each of the 26 statements. Choose 5 for most agree / most applicable, down to 1 for least agree / least applicable:

Although there is no overall time limit, do not spend more than a few seconds thinking about any one question as it is best to give the first answer that comes to mind.

Be truthful to yourself and give the answer best suited to your beliefs or how you perceive yourself.

Even though you may be doubtful about some specific question, this should still be answered by choosing the option that you believe to be the closest to you own personality, or how you would be likely to react to a certain situation given the choice.

Test One

Subject: Success Factor

Question 1

It is of paramount importance to me that I am a success in my chosen profession.

5   4   3   2   1

Question 2

I do not find it difficult to focus on one thing at a time.

5   4   3   2   1

Question 3

I am continually looking forward to, and planning for, the future.

5   4   3   2   1

Question 4

In life you make your own luck

5   4   3   2   1

Question 5

I am continually setting myself goals.

5   4   3   2   1

Question 6

I am most strongly motivated by my own personal desires.

5   4   3   2   1

Question 7

I am a stronger person mentally than I was 5 years ago.

5   4   3   2   1

Question 8

I am a very tenacious.

5   4   3   2   1

Question 9

The harder you work at something the better you become.

5   4   3   2   1

Question 10

I know where I want to be in 5 years time.

5   4   3   2   1

Question 11

I would never let my hobby interfere with my career.

5   4   3   2   1

Question 12

I am continually on the lookout to grasp any opportunity that may present itself

5   4   3   2   1

Question 13

I always strive to see every job, or task, that I undertake through to completion

5   4   3   2   1

Question 14

I always try to make the right contacts and impress the right people.

5   4   3   2   1

Question 15

It is always too soon to quit.

5   4   3   2   1

Question 16

It is always possible to overcome social barriers

5   4   3   2   1

Question 17

I would not hesitate to change my career in order to achieve my goals

5   4   3   2   1

Question 18

Hard work is a means to an end.

    5   4   3   2   1

Question 19

I am not afraid of failure.

    5   4   3   2   1

Question 20

I cannot describe myself as a good loser.

    5   4   3   2   1

Question 21

I am not stuck in a rut.

    5   4   3   2   1

Question 22

Every day is an exciting new challenge.

    5   4   3   2   1

Question 23

I would describe myself as a very shrewd person.

    5   4   3   2   1

Question 24

Character and persistence are more of a key to success than a high level of intelligence

    5   4   3   2   1

Question 25

I can be ruthless when it comes to getting what I want.

5   4   3   2   1

Question 26

It is important to enjoy whatever you are doing.

5   4   3   2   1

Assessment:

Total score 115 - 130	Exceptionally high success factor
Total score 105 -114	Very high success factor
Total score 95 -104	High success factor
Total score 85 - 94	Well above average success factor
Total score 75 - 84	Above average success factor
Total score 60 - 74	Average success factor
Total score 50 - 59	Below average success factor
Total score below 50	Low success factor

There is no single definition of success, as what is considered to be success by one individual may differ considerably for another. Generally, however, success means achieving the things in life that we set out to achieve, and is the positive results of all our efforts.

For many people success means being happy and contented, and holding down a steady job to provide a regular income and security for their family. For others power, status and monetary wealth are their definition of success and in business they will not rest until they are at the top of the corporate ladder.

For whatever degree of success to which they aspire, successful people tend to set themselves goals. Such goals, which should provide meaningful, yet realistic challenges, can be anything you want or need, and take you from where you are now to where you wish to be in the long-term or even short-term future. The goals you set can, however, only be effective providing you know what you want from life and take the necessary action to achieve these goals. You must also be flexible enough to change what you are doing, if this is necessary in order to achieve your goals.

It is necessary always to strike the right balance in order to reach most of the goals you have set out to achieve both in your personal and working life. If you do not strike this right balance, then one part of your life is likely to suffer at the expense of another.

A keyword on the road to success is persistence. Successful people overcome many hurdles before achieving their aspirations. It is important to view any failures positively and learn from them. Each challenge that we face should make us stronger mentally and every failure should make us more determined to succeed. It is important to quickly turn any losing situation into a winning one and regain control.

Keywords on the road to success:

Positive, motivation, adaptability, resilience, persistence, commitment, energy, self-confidence, diligence.

Test Two

Subject: Self -Confidence Factor

Question 1

I am a great believer in the power of positive thinking

| 5 | 4 | 3 | 2 | 1 |

Question 2

I feel very good about myself

| 5 | 4 | 3 | 2 | 1 |

Question 3

It is not necessary to conform in order to be accepted

| 5 | 4 | 3 | 2 | 1 |

Question 4

I would relish the opportunity to take part in a political debate on television

| 5 | 4 | 3 | 2 | 1 |

Question 5

I very rarely feel sad or depressed.

 5   4   3   2   1

Question 6

I am not backward at coming forward.

 5   4   3   2   1

Question 7

I am very good at selling myself.

 5   4   3   2   1

Question 8

I am very self-reliant.

 5   4   3   2   1

Question 9

I never put myself down.

 5   4   3   2   1

Question 10

I am very much in control of my own life.

 5   4   3   2   1

Question 11

I never worry about living up to the standards of others.

 5   4   3   2   1

Question 12

I would not be at all nervous about meeting someone very famous.

5   4   3   2   1

Question 13

I do not need the approval of others in order to feel good about myself

5   4   3   2   1

Question 14

I would never be afraid of standing up and making my point of view known at a public meeting.

5   4   3   2   1

Question 15

I always have the courage of my own convictions.

5   4   3   2   1

Question 16

If I do not agree with someone I say so.

5   4   3   2   1

Question 17

It is fun from time to time to live dangerously.

5   4   3   2   1

Question 18

I never worry about my appearance.

5   4   3   2   1

Question 19

I have always been able to bounce back quickly after adversity.

5   4   3   2   1

Question 20

I am not afraid of taking risks.

5   4   3   2   1

Question 21

The thought of making a speech in front of a large audience does not worry me.

5   4   3   2   1

Question 22

I will achieve that which is important to me.

5   4   3   2   1

Question 23

I never feel self-conscious in public places.

5   4   3   2   1

Question 24

It is essential to set high yet realistic goals.

5   4   3   2   1

Question 25

I set my own personal standards.

5   4   3   2   1

I accept myself for what I am.

      5   4   3   2   1

Assessment:

Total score 115 - 130	Exceptionally high self-confidence factor
Total score 105 -114	Very high self-confidence factor
Total score 95 -104	High self-confidence factor
Total score 85 - 94	Well above average self-confidence factor
Total score 75 - 84	Above average self-confidence factor
Total score 60 - 74	Average self-confidence factor
Total score 50 - 59	Below average self-confidence factor
Total score below 50	Low self-confidence factor

Self-confidence is assuredness and self-reliance in one's own abilities.

This part of a person's character manifests itself in several ways. Self-confident people, for example, very rarely feel unsure of themselves and preoccupied with negative self thoughts, or put themselves down. Nor are they often sad, depressed or lonely. At the same time, because they do not feel the need to conform in order to be accepted, self-confident people are not excessively dependent on others to feel good about themselves. They are willing to risk the disapproval of others because of the confidence they have in themselves and the ability to accept themselves for what they are.

Self-confident people have the ability to develop an attitude in which they are able, to a great extent, to take control of their own life and stand up for their own rights and aspirations in today's sometimes intimidating world, but at the same time keeping these aspirations realistic.

Self-confidence need not apply to all respects of a person's lifestyle. Because self-confidence also means the ability to take a realistic view of themselves, some individuals will have total confidence in some aspect of their lives, such as sporting prowess, but other aspects in which they do not feel so confident, such as academic achievement.

Being self-confident does not, therefore, mean being able to do everything. It does mean, however, that when sometimes their aspirations are not fulfilled, self-confident people continue to adopt a positive attitude and make the best of their situation. At all times it is important to keep a sense of reality and be wary of over-confidence to the extent that others perceive them as brash or cocky.

The following are some strategies that can be adopted, and worked at, for developing a greater degree of self-confidence.

- Focus on your achievements and any talents you possess by evaluating and emphasising your strengths.

- Give yourself credit for everything you try to achieve. Even if you fail, give yourself credit for trying. View any failure as a learning experience and as achieving personal growth.

- Do not be afraid of taking risks. Regard risk taking as a chance to grasp new opportunities.

- Never be afraid of change.

- Accept yourself for what you are at the same time balancing this with the need to improve. Accept there is no such thing as perfection.

- Do not try to please everyone at the same time

- Learn to self-evaluate and take charge of your own life. Do not focus too much on the unrealistic aspirations or standards of others such as parents. Instead, focus on how you feel about yourself, your lifestyle and your own aspirations.

Test Three

Subject: Leadership Factor

Question 1

Scathing criticism does not upset me.

    5   4   3   2   1

Question 2

All members of a team should be stimulated by being given responsibility

    5   4   3   2   1

Question 3

I would prefer a less secure job with high prospects of promotion, rather than a steady and secure job with no prospects of promotion.

5   4   3   2   1

Question 4

I am often asked for my advice.

5   4   3   2   1

Question 5

I regard myself as something of a trend setter.

5   4   3   2   1

Question 6

Camaraderie is one of the most essential factors in building a successful team.

5   4   3   2   1

Question 7

I prefer to do my own thing, rather than keep up to date with the latest fashions.

5   4   3   2   1

Question 8

It is important to help others to see the best in themselves.

5   4   3   2   1

Question 9

I am an enthusiastic organiser.

5   4   3   2   1

Question 10

To understand people you must first know yourself.

5   4   3   2   1

Question 11

Life is very much a team game.

5   4   3   2   1

Question 12

In order to get the best out of people it is preferable to support them rather than drive them

5   4   3   2   1

Question 13

I always try to keep up to date with the latest technology

5   4   3   2   1

Question 14

Charisma is a more important leadership quality than experience.

5   4   3   2   1

Question 15

Never be afraid to admit you are wrong.

5   4   3   2   1

Question 16

I am stimulated by the thought of being in charge.

5   4   3   2   1

Question 17

I do not look up to people in authority

5   4   3   2   1

Question 18

I need to be in control rather than going with the flow.

5   4   3   2   1

Question 19

There will always be a need for strong leadership in society.

5   4   3   2   1

Question 20

I would prefer to be a committee chairman rather than just a member of that committee.

5   4   3   2   1

Question 21

I am a good team player.

5   4   3   2   1

Question 22

I have the ability to be at the top of my chosen career or profession.

5   4   3   2   1

Question 23

I pride myself at being able to keep a cool head under pressure.

    5   4   3   2   1

Question 24

I am a great believer in regular staff appraisals.

    5   4   3   2   1

Question 25

The greater the challenge the greater the effort.

    5   4   3   2   1

Question 26

I have no difficulty in totally absorbing myself in my work.

    5   4   3   2   1

Assessment:

Total score 115 – 130	Exceptionally high leadership factor
Total score 105 –114	Very high leadership factor
Total score 95 –104	High leadership factor
Total score 85 – 94	Well above average leadership factor
Total score 75 – 84	Above average leadership factor
Total score 60 – 74	Average leadership factor
Total score 50 – 59	Below average leadership factor
Total score below 50	Low leadership factor

Some people do not aspire to leadership and are happy to go with the tide and let others take the initiative, whilst others do aspire to leadership and possess the necessary qualities required to be a successful leader.

A definition of a leader is anyone who holds the position of dominance, authority or influence in a group, or team, and is, in psychology, applied to someone who possesses the necessary qualities to become such a leader.

There are many different qualities necessary to be a successful leader which is dependant to a great extent on the type of leadership situation. A great military leader such as Napoleon, for example, must have organizational skills as well as the ability to motivate his troops, and the same can be said of many leaders in business settings, or team leaders within a business organization.

To be a success in many walks of life is not necessarily to be a success individually, indeed in the majority of instances, success is achieved as part of a team.

We are all, in some way in our life, part of a team; in fact life itself is to a great extent a team game. Whether it is a small team or a large team, and in whatever setting, team growth can also lead to individual growth in which we can all move forward by learning new concepts, increasing our skills, broadening our minds and sustaining motivation.

A good leader is required to understand the importance of the team's purpose and challenges but also needs to focus on maintaining its camaraderie, responsibility and growth.

Both teams and individuals are stimulated by responsibility and it is necessary for team leaders to create the right conditions in which the team is able to motivate itself to take these responsibilities seriously and to recognise the need for team members to pull together to achieve their objectives. While a team does consist of individuals, it is only when these individuals pull together towards a common goal that the team can really be effective.

Section Three
Problem Solving

Section Three

Problem Solving:

There is a story, perhaps apocryphal, about two equally qualified graduate students who were interviewed for a position at one of America's largest and best-known companies.

Towards the end of their interview both graduates were given a large geometric puzzle cut into several hundred pieces and asked to solve it within 30 minutes.

They were timed and, under intense pressure, the first graduate started to panic and sweat profusely, and as a result made little or no progress with the puzzle.
He did not get the job offer.

The second graduate took a much more analytical approach. Remaining calm, he looked at the puzzle from several different angles and made a number of notes, starting off by saying that he could not solve the puzzle within 30 minutes but that he estimated it could be solved within 2 hours, after which he went on to detail the reasoning process that he would use to solve the puzzle.

It turned out that this was exactly what the interviewer was hoping to learn. The second graduate received a job offer, is still working with the same company and carving out a successful career.

Many companies are now adopting this unconventional approach as part of the interviewing process and this latest twist in hiring techniques includes the setting of brainteaser type puzzles in order to test for mental agility and to see how the candidate is able to handle unexpected pressure.

In such a situation the most successful candidates will be able to demonstrate their composure and creativity and their ability to think logically by analysing and deconstructing a problem and, if necessary, to ask appropriate and relevant questions.

The following are some typical questions that have been asked of candidates in the past few years by large multi national companies. They will give you a flavour of the type of question with which you could suddenly be faced during the job interview process.

You will find full explanations, where necessary, in the answers section on page 147, together with some pertinent questions for which you would be given credit for asking, all of which should give you an indication of the type of thought processes necessary in tackling this type of question.

For questions 1 - 5 you are allowed 3 minutes work on each question.

Question 1

You are on the road to Honestville with no map and no way of knowing the correct route to take. You come to a fork in the road. One road leads to Honestville, where everyone always tells the truth, but the other road leads to Shamtown, where everyone always lies.

At the fork is a man from one of these towns, but you do not know which one.

You are allowed to ask him one question in order to discover the way to Honestville. What question should you ask him?

Question 2

You are at a car boot sale and are planning to sell an item which you know you can sell for £50.00.

At the next stall the vendor brings out an identical item which he marks up at £10.00. What is your best strategy in this situation?

Question 3

You have eight coins, identical in appearance, one of which is a forgery and weighs slightly less than the rest.

Using a Libra type two-arm weigh scale, and with just two weighing operations, find the counterfeit coin.

Question 4

Why are manhole covers round?

Question 5

Calculate the number of degrees between the hour hand and the minute hand of a non-digital clock that shows the time as 15 minutes past 3.

Whilst the following two questions may seem somewhat obscure, or even bizarre, they should be taken seriously as what the interviewer is looking for, above all, is not necessarily the correct answer, but your line of thinking.

You are allowed 10 minutes work on each question.

Question 6

How many barbers are there in the city of Chicago?

Question 7

How many golf balls does it take to fill an Olympic sized swimming pool?

Although the next two puzzles are somewhat complex in nature, they should still be approached in a confident, logical and structured manner. Even if you do not arrive at the correct answers within the set time limit you can still impress your interviewer by showing that you are capable of thinking correctly and working towards a correct solution.

You are allowed 30 minutes work on each question

Question 8

Three hitchhikers embark on a journey in China and each set off from the same place at 12 noon on the same day. The following is an account of their progress on the first day.

First traveller:

Journeyed by truck for 1 hour at 30 mph, by foot for 3hours at 3.5 mph and by horse and cart for 4 hours at 10mph

Second traveller:

Journeyed by horse and cart for 2 hours at 10 mph, by truck for 1.5 hours at 40 mph and by foot for 3 hours at 3.5 mph

Third traveller:

Journeyed by foot for 3 hours at 3.5 mph, by horse and cart for 3 hours at 10 mph and by truck for 2 hours at 30 mph.

Who overtook whom and at what time?

(You should assume there was minimal waiting time for each of the travellers in their transition from any one form of travel to another.)

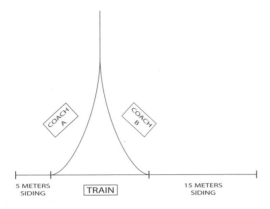

The train is 10 metres long and the coaches are each 5 metres long. All other dimensions other than those shown can be any length.

By shunting you have to reverse the positions of coach A and coach B, and return the train to its starting point.

Section Four
How to Approach
a Psychometric Test

How to approach a Psychometric test

Human resources people are aliens (with apologies to *men in black*)

The above comment was made by a candidate who had recently taken a battery of psychometric tests when attending a job interview for the position of computer programmer.

Sometimes, however, it is necessary to look at the recruiting process from an employer's point of view in order to understand why this type of testing is becoming more and more prevalent. Because the recruiting and training of staff can be such a long and expensive process, it is important that the company get it right first time, and the use of psychological testing, which may be addressed to any aspect of our intellectual or emotional make-up, including personality, attitude and intelligence, is a valuable tool that they have at their disposal to enable them to make the correct recruiting decision.

So, although to many job applicants, the use of such testing may seem to be something of a distasteful procedure, the process should not be negatively viewed in this way and it should also be remembered that you never get a second chance to make a good first impression.

Applicants should take the positive view that this form of testing gives them the opportunity to demonstrate to the employer that they are the best person for the job, and that as a result the right applicant will be chosen on merit.

In any case, an organisation will not found its entire decision on the basis of an individual's test results. Psychometric testing is a part of the selection process, and is not a substitute for interviewing. Testing, in fact, works best when combined with a face-to-face talk.

Many companies like the red carpet, face-to-face treatment in which the job is made highly appealing in order to attract the right applicants, however, even this type of approach will usually be done in conjunction with psychometric testing.

Having now adopted a positive attitude, as well as familiarising yourself with the type of questions you are likely to encounter on IQ tests and practising on this type of question over and over again - practise makes perfect - it is also essential that you approach an IQ test confidently and systematically and without getting into a state of panic. It is obviously advisable to carry out some research into the type of question you may encounter, however, it is also very advantageous to be in the right frame of mind. It is likely that you will have some anxiety symptoms prior to taking any kind of test, in fact a certain degree of anxiety, or butterflies in the stomach can be helpful in a test situation because it shows that you are concentrating and focusing your energies on the task ahead. On the other hand, if you are overly anxious, this is likely to affect your performance adversely.

When taking the actual test it may be helpful to bear in mind as many of the following points as possible:

· try to get a good night's sleep beforehand

· do not take the test on an empty stomach

· arrive in good time for the test and, above all, don't dash in at the last minute flustered and wound up

· read the instructions to each test carefully

· bear in mind that the more questions you usually answer the higher you score, so work as quickly, but as carefully as possible.

· focus your attention on the job in hand - avoid all distractions

· make sure you are comfortable

· if you have a practice or instructional stage before the test proper pay attention to this very carefully, irrespective of how trivial or obvious some of the points being made by the administrator may appear. At this stage do not be afraid to ask any questions of the administrator. Also remember that any instructions given are necessary to ensure that everyone takes the test under exactly the same conditions, so listen carefully to the administrator's brief and ask any questions prior to the commencement of the test.

·try to relax, stay calm

· don't panic!! If you panic you may begin to lose confidence in your own ability to answer the most obvious questions. Although it is easy to say Don't panic, when faced with any task or situation which involves pressure, it is not that easy to do. Too much time and too little time to do it is a scenario that is familiar to most of us. If, however, you are able to discipline yourself to approach any such circumstance in a logical, calm and structured fashion, it is surprising how the task becomes much less daunting.

· work quickly and accurately, but do not rush.

· make sure you put your answers in the correct place

· keep your eye on the time

· do not spend too long on any one question, either come back to it at the end of the test if there is time remaining, or make an educated or intuitive guess

· double check each answer quickly

· do not be afraid of any one type of question

· approach the questions systematically and analytically

· bear in mind that in many tests, questions progressively get harder

· keep your eye on the time and try to pace yourself

· if you have time to spare at the end of the test, do not just sit back with an air of satisfaction, but rather use the extra time to have a quick review of your answers. You do not get any extra marks for finishing early, also we have all been guilty of slips of the pen at one time or another and this may well be one of those occasions.

As in the case of many new experiences, one of the main keys to success is understanding. By obtaining an understanding of the testing process and its purpose, and by the adopting of a positive attitude towards this type of testing, you will increase your chances of success when attending an interview. At the same time this will help to ensure that you make a positive start to your career by being placed with a company, and in a job, to which you are best suited, and this will thus increase your potential for ultimately achieving career success in business or in a business environment.

Answers

General Ability Test

1. C- adept, effect

2. 6852   5741

3. D- The combined age of Peter and Paul is 56 years

4. 420: 7 x 6 x 5 = 210. 1 x 1 x 0.5 = 0.5. 210/0.5 = 420

5. £3.50
   £3.50 + £4.75 = 8.25. £8.25 x 5 = £41.25.
   £41.25 - £37.75 = £3.50

6. B. except, admittance, admission

7. 1400: 168/12 x 100

8. f, e, a, c, b, d

9. During the course of each working day the call centre handled hundreds of enquiries from customers and potential customers.

10. 7.5 hours
    100 miles @ 20mph = 5 hours
    100 miles @ 40 mph = 2.5 hours

11. A- looking across and down, each row and column contains a black inner circle, a horizontal line and a vertical line.

12. Jones £42,000, Green £84,000 and Brown £154,000`
    Total investment = £200,000
    Jones   15% of £280,000 = £42,000
    Green   30% of £280,000 = £84,000
    Brown   55% of £280,000 = £154,000
                100%   £280,000

13. executable

14. B. 3.937

15. 27.5 cm
    (32/6.4) x 5.5

---

16. 5745 spectators
     38300 x 0.85 = 32555.
     38300 - 32555 = 5745

17. metre

18. G- association of ideas

19. The police decided to prosecute and let the judicial process run its course, knowing that the defendant would have recourse to appeal at any sentence passed.

20. 32
     27 + 64 = 91. 123 - 91 = 32

21. B, D, A, C

22. 8.75 days:
     the five men take 5 x 14 = 70 days to build the house. Eight men, therefore, build the house in 70/8 = 8.75 days.

23. A

24. Yes.
     7/25 = 0.28
     648/2418 = 0.268

25. B- 6.452   (929.03/144)

26. predetermine

27. E- the white dot moves 90° clockwise, and the black dot alternates between two positions

28. 8kg
     4 x 5 = 20   4 x 9 = 36
     2 x 8 = 16
              36

29. pipe

30. C- statics

31. twenty

32. 20%
    Myself 18 out of 30 = 60%   My sister 6 out of 15 = 40%

33. abearing, Abednego, Aberdare, Aberdeen, aberrate, abessive, abetment, abettals, abetters, abetting, abettors, abeyancy

34. D

35. B

36. The right side of the brain reconstructs a whole pattern out of individual pieces, at the same time giving rise to new ideas and concepts.

37. 37.5 hours
    7.25 hours per day x 6 = 43.5 less 6 hours for lunch

38. C- looking across and down, lines are carried forward to the third pentagon from the first two pentagons, except where two lines appear in the same position, in which case they are cancelled out.

39. The correct use of punctuation when writing business letters is essential to convey the writer's exact meaning.

40. 30%
    Total of ages = 350, i.e average age of the ten people = 35
    Three people are older than 35, or 30%

Assessment:

Each completely correct answer scores one point

36 - 40	Exceptional
31 - 35	Excellent
25 - 30	Very Good
19 - 24	Good
12 - 18	Average

General Intelligence IQ Test

1. book, opera

2. 1- each column totals 20, 18, 16, 14, 12

3. B- the small circle at the top rolls along increasing in size until it reaches the corner then decreases in size again. The circle with the line rolls in the opposite direction, decreasing in size until it reaches the corner after which it increases in size again.

4. isolated

5. a minus sign

6. D- the small circle with the two dots rotates 90° clockwise and moves to the right of the large circle, the circle with the black dot moves to the bottom of the large circle, and the small empty circle moves into the middle of the large circle.

7. augment

8. 5- 36/4 = 9, 85/5 = 17, 12/6 = 2, 56/7 = 8, 48/8 = 6, 72/9 = 8, 40/10 = 4, therefore, 55/11 = 5.

9. Building- it is a general term, the rest are places where people live.

10. 446: deduct 29 each time

11. D- the first three figures are being repeated

12. formula

13. 5- in each set the second two numbers are the product of the first two numbers. Therefore, 5 x 9 = 45

14. interim

15 party

16. 24:

$$(9 - 5) \times \frac{(7 + 11)}{3}$$

17. E- looking across and down lines are carried forward from the first two squares to the third square, except where lines appear in both these squares in the same position, in which case they are cancelled out.

18. meditative

19. order

20. D- in each row and column the dot appears once in one circle, once in two circles and once in three circles.

21. Sally = 39, Tony = 26, Maria = 13
    39 + 13 = 26 x 2
    26 + 13 = 39

22. disinclined

23. vegetable, moss

24. 0- the numbers in the second block of four are two less than the numbers in the same position in the first block. The numbers in the third block are three less than those in the second block.

25. BEACH
    SNUGLY   LUNAR   ARTFUL
    PAELLA   BEACH   CHERUB
    32   12345   45   1

26. C- the rest are the same figure rotated.

27. C- optimal

28. slavery

29. C- looking across the numbers progress +5, -2, +5. Looking down they progress, -2, +5, -2

30. B- looking across the dotted line moves left to right. Looking down the dotted line moves top to bottom.

31. CABLE
    OWNER   WISER   SHINE
    SCORE   CABLE   BRAWL
    1   5   12345   3 2 4

32. announce, claim

33. 105- in another two years we will be 2 x 3 = 6 years older. 99 + 6 = 105

34. B- looking across jump one letter in the alphabet. Looking down, jump two letters

35. D- reversing the first analogy, the top circle moves to the right, the middle circle moves to the left and the bottom circle moves to the middle.

36. H- TsrQpoNmlKjiH

37. 96314

38. store

39. 2- $\frac{7 \times 4}{14}$

40. A. intangible
    B. flagship
    C. flotation
    D. monopoly
    E. logo
    F. incorporate

Assessment:

Each completely correct answer scores one point

36 - 40	Exceptional
31 - 35	Excellent
25 - 30	Very Good
19 - 24	Good
12 - 18	Average

Numerical Aptitude

Number Sequence Test

1. 48- add 16 each time

2. 21- add 0,1,2,3,4,5,6

3. 364- deduct 101, 103, 105, 107, 109, 111

4. 26- there are two separate sequences running alternately - 5 plus 2, 3, 4, 5, and 6 plus 2,4,6,8

5. 0- +1, -2, +3, -4, +5, -6

6. 21- +0.5, 1.5, 4.5, 13.5 i.e. the amount added is multiplied by 3 each time

7. 66.5- deduct 6.7 each time

8. 55- there are two alternate sequences: 10 plus 3, 6, 9, 12 and 100 minus 3, 6, 12, 24

9. 62.5- the amount deducted increases by 2.5 each time

10. 94- multiply by three and add 1 each time

Assessment:

4 - 5	Average
6 - 7	Good
8	Very Good
9 - 10	Exceptional

Calculation Test

1. 3

2. Joe 27, Mo 36, Flo 48

3. 4

   $$\frac{8+20}{7}$$

4. 6 (3 x 2)

5. 45 minutes- 11.15 less 1 hour = 10.15. 8 am + 135 minute (3 x 45) = 10.15

6. 6

   4 + 2 = 6

   1 + 2 = 3

7. 90 (5 x 18)

8. 18, 19, 20, 21, 22

   As the numbers are consecutive, the numbers in the triangles must be either 18 and 19 or 19 and 18. As the numbers in the square total 60, the numbers must be increasing from left to right.

9.

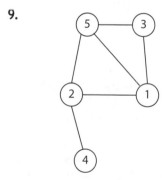

10. Mary 168, Tony 112, Frank 56.

Assessment:

4 - 5	Average
6 - 7	Good
8	Very Good
9 - 10	Exceptional

Calculation And Logic Test

1. 4- 12 x 3 = 36. 36/9 = 4

2. 49- in each line and column add the first three numbers to arrive at the end number.

3. 1- take the total of the two numbers above and below the middle number and deduct from the total of the two numbers to the left and right of the middle number. So, 9 + 5 and 3 + 11 both equal 14, and 5 + 8 and 7 + 6 both equal 13. The difference between 14 and 13 is 1.

4. 14- add the numbers in the same segments in the left and right circles to obtain the number in the corresponding segment in the middle circle.

5. 29- in each set the total of the numbers reading down is 50 and the total of the numbers reading across is 100. So, 14 + 29 + 7 = 50, and 35 + 29 + 36 = 100

6. 37- (37 + 11)/2 = 24. Similarly (9+7)/2 = 8

7.

A	B	C	D	E
7	4	9	3	2
5	16	6	9	13
22	11	29	18	22
40	51	33	44	40
84	73	91	80	84

A + C = B (on the line below).
Similarly D + E = A,
B + E = C,
A + E = D
and B + C = E

8. 57- in each row and column add the first two numbers to obtain the third number and add the second and third numbers to obtain the fourth number.

9. 12- the numbers in the triangles total 43, as do the numbers in the circles, squares and ellipses.

10. 3- the total of the numbers in the shaded segments is twice as many as the total of the numbers in the unshaded segments.

Assessment:

4 - 5	Average
6 - 7	Good
8	Very Good
9 - 10	Exceptional

Numerical Matrix Test

1. B- looking across the numbers progress + 3.
   Looking down they progress +4

2. D- looking across lines in turn progress +2, +3, +4, +5.
   Looking down each column lines progress in turn +5, +6, +7, +8

3. A- looking across each line progresses +1, +2, +3.
   Looking down, each column progresses +3, +2, +1

4. C- looking across each line progresses +4, +2, +1.
   Looking down, each column progresses +1, +2, +4

5. B- looking across alternate numbers progress +1 and +3.
   Looking down alternate numbers progress +3 and +1

6. B- looking across numbers decrease by 3.
   Looking down numbers decrease by 4

7. D- looking across numbers progress +1, +2, +1.
   Looking down they progress +2, +1, +2

8. C- looking across the numbers in the first row increase by 3, in the second row they increase by 5, in the third row by 7, in the fourth row by 2 and in the fifth row by 4

9. A- looking along the first row the numbers increase by 2, then back along the second row they increase by 3, then along the third row by 4, back along the fourth row by 5 and finally along the fifth row they increase by 6

10. C- looking along the first row the numbers decrease by 1, then back along the second row they increase by 2, then along the third row they decrease by 3, back along the fourth row they increase by 4, and finally along the fifth row they decrease by 5

Assessment:

4 -	5	Average
6 -	7	Good
	8	Very Good
9 -	10	Exceptional

Eclectic Numerical Test (Calculation And Logic)

1. C- 50% profit

2. B and D- 33 1/3% profit

3. 30, 70- there are two interwoven sequences. The sequence starting at 0 proceeds + 7.5, and the alternate sequence starting at 100 proceeds - 7.5

4. 7 per minute
   Between 10am and 11am, 300 calls were received. There were 40% more between 2pm and 3pm i.e. 420, or 7 (420/60) per minute.

5. D. 21.42
   £28.00 less 10% = £25.20, and £25.20 less 15% = £21.42

6. £16750.00
   £45,000 @ 23% = £ 10350.00
   £20,000 @ 32% = £ 6400,00
   £ 16750.00

7. 90- deduct 1, 2, 3, 4, 5, 6

8. Player C with an aggregate of 3,788,340 over player A with 2,375,440 and player B with 3,075,200

9. Player B- 792,600 in game 1 and 2,282,600 in game 2

10. 513,300

11. 1 hour 39 minutes

12. 66- Combined age in 12 years = 94.
    4 x 12 = 48, therefore, combined age now is 94 - 48 = 46
    In 5 years time the combined age is, therefore, 46 + 20 (4 x 5) = 66

13. 60- 4 x 3 x 5`

14. 54- add 3.6 then double, add 3.6 then double etc

15. £7.50
    £100.00 less 3/5 (£60.00) = £40.00.
    £40.00 less 60% = £16.00
    £16.00 less £8.50 = £7.50

16. £83.20

   Train £56.75, taxi £56.75 - 32.85 = £23.90, bus £23.90 - 21.35 = £2.55
   Total £83.20

17. 11, 64- there are two alternate sequences; 1,2,4,8,16,32 and 1,3,5,7,9

18. 900-

   5/16 + 10/16 (5/8) = 15/16.
   1/16, therefore, = 90, and 10/16 (900) had bought just clothing

19. 117- add 39 each time

20. 82- (6 x 9) + (7 x 4)

21. D- looking across the numbers progress + 2, + 3, + 4. Looking down the
   numbers progress +4, +3, +2

22. 535- 417 + 286 = 703 and 286 + 249 = 535

23. 12, 13- +5, +1 repeated

24. 78, 74.5: -3.5, -7.5 repeated

25. 72- the number formed by the two middle digits is the product of
   the first and last digits.

Assessment:

8 - 11	Average
12 - 17	Good
18 - 22	Very Good
23 - 25	Exceptional

Eclectic Numerical Test (Calculation, Logic and Lateral Thinking)

1. 1.5

2. 41 minutes-
   11.19 less 57 minutes = 10.22 9am plus 82 minutes (41 x 2) = 10.22

3. 97.5 lbs.
   100 - 35% = 65.
   65 - 20% = 52
   52 - 25% = 39

   39% of 250 lbs = 97.5

4. B- 698 : 62
   (6 x 9) + 8 = 62

5. E- 6739:1312:43
   6 + 7 = 13, 3 + 9 = 12; and 1 + 3 = 4, 1 + 2 = 3

6. 8172- 3 x 9 x 3 = 81 and 4 x 2 x 9 = 72

7. 148620- reverse the first four digits and then the last two.

8. 1.7- x1, x2, x3, x4, x5

9. 27- (32 + 14) - 19

10. 96- 297/594 = 1/2. 1/2 x 1/2 = 1/4. 1/4 x 384 = 96

11. 28- looking across and down, multiply the first two numbers together and divide by 4

12. 5   2   4   3   1   or   1   3   4   2   5

13. B- 581321: 5 + 8 = 13; 8 + 13 = 21

14. 15.75 sq.metres:
    15 x 11 =   165
    5.5 x 3.5 = 19.25
                184.25

    200.00 less 184.25 = 15.75

---

15. grapefruit 180, apples 270, oranges 360
    1 part = 90: 810/9 (2+3+4)

16. 47- there are two alternate sequences; +3,+6,+12, +24 and -3,-6,-12, -24

17. £1.70
    A pack of eight costs £2.48 or £0.31 each in the pack. If bought individually they cost £0.34 (3 pence each more). £0.34 x 5 = £1.70

18. 15%

19.

A	B	C	D	E
4	6	3	2	1
10	7	8	4	3
17	18	11	11	7
35	28	29	18	18
63	64	46	47	36

A + C = B in the line below.
Similarly B + D = C,
C + E = D,
A + B = A
and D + E = E

20.

		95		
	48	47		
	26	22	25	
14	12	10	15	
5	9	3	7	8

21. 45- Reducing everything to sixteenths;1/16 of 240 = 15.
    4/16 + 6/16 + 3/16 = 13/16. this leaves 3/16 who took it black = 45

22. 102: (3 x 17) x 2

23. 7: in each block of four numbers, opposite numbers total the same.
    So, 1 + 13 = 7 + 7

24. 8- the numbers in the second square are the numbers formed in each line of the first square multiplied by 2   . So 349 x 2 = 698 and 284 x 2 = 568

25. 4- The numbers in the third line are the numbers in the first line reversed plus 1.
    The numbers in the fifth line are the numbers in the third line reversed plus 1.

The numbers in the fourth line are the numbers in the second line reversed plus 1.

The numbers in the sixth line are the numbers in the fourth line reversed plus 1.

Assessment:

8 - 11	Average
12 - 17	Good
18 - 22	Very Good
23 - 25	Exceptional

Verbal Aptitude

Classification Test

1. demonic: it means ghoulish, the rest meaning ghostly

2. guileful: it means crafty, the rest mean learned

3. independent: it means single-handed, the rest mean single-minded

4. dissimulating: it means phoney, the rest mean phlegmatic

5. ladder: the rest are for sitting on

6. polemic: it means controversial, the rest mean thinkable

7. quantity: it could be any unspecified number, large or small, the rest mean a large quantity

8. sierra: it refers to mountains, the rest are grassland

9. dextral: it means right hand, the rest mean left hand

10. simper: this is shy, affected speech, the rest mean to speak aimlessly and at tedious length

Assessment:

4 - 5	Average
6 - 7	Good
8	Very Good
9 - 10	Exceptional

Synonym Test

1. abatement

2. assign

3. taxing

4. profusion

5. recondite

6. B- hibernal

7. E- suffrage

8. cancellation, abrogation

9. envision, anticipate

10. wry, askew

Assessment:

4 - 5	Average
6 - 7	Good
8	Very Good
9 - 10	Exceptional

Antonym Test

1. solemn

2. reluctant

3. paucity

4. liberation

5. heighten

6. pastel, vibrant

7. real, feigned

8. withdrawn, accessible

9. adjacent, remote

10. asset, encumbrance

Assessment:

4 - 5	Average
6 - 7	Good
8	Very Good
9 - 10	Exceptional

Analogy Test

1. mother, brother

2. star, dagger

3. thousand, thousandth

4. tank, canal

5. priority, examples

6. lessor, lessee

7. quadrilateral

8. capacity

9. file

10. iron

Assessment:

4 - 5	Average
6 - 7	Good
8	Very Good
9 - 10	Exceptional

Eclectic Verbal Ability Test I

1. The combination of learning and memory is the basis of all our knowledge and abilities and is what enables us to consider the past, exist in the present and plan for the future.

2. C

3. Bees manufacture their honey in hives that are filled with hexagon shapes, simply because hexagons fit together with no loss of space.

4. C

5. D

6. Paris, soon

7. notion, idea

8. QPY- N moves forward three places in the alphabet to Q, S moves three places back to P and V moves three places forward to Y

9. P- ABcDefGhijKlmnoP

10. D
    I
    N
    AbCdE
    BcdEfgH
    CdefGhijK
    DefghIjklmN

11. diameter, hypotenuse

12. punitive, vindictive

13. mundane, interesting

14. C

15. B

16. discreet

17. C

18. expand, wane

19. D

20. affable

21. bland

22. outwit

23. ABDGKP- miss one letter, then two letters etc. So, AB, ABcD, ABDefG, ABDGhijK, ABDGKlmnoP

24. propel, launch

25. just

Assessment:

8 - 11	Average
12 - 17	Good
18 - 22	Very Good
23 - 25	Exceptional

Eclectic Verbal Ability Test II

1. B. adhere- each word commences with the first two letters of the preceding word

2. D

3. soften-

FOREST	(SOFTEN)	UNIONS
3 5 4	1 2 3 4 5 6	6 2 1
RANKLE	(EUREKA)	SALUTE

4. B

5. travel

6. C and E

7. legendary

8. any time now

9. chestnut, auburn, hazel

10. ILOYSN = nosily

11. baa lain = Albania. The B countries are Barbados, Bhutan and Bulgaria

12. indolent, sluggish

13. sceptical, convinced

14. consortium, conglomerate

15. language

16. head over heels

17. pass: underpass, passage

18. G

19. occupied, deserted

20. All can be suffixed or prefixed with happy; happy event, trigger happy, happy medium, happy landing, slap happy

21. acephalist, acerbitude, acervative, acervuline, acetarious, acetimeter, acetometer, acetonemia

22. paragon, archetype

23. sugared: the vowels AEIOU are being repeated in the same order

24. C

25. gave: gave horn is an anagram of overhang.
    Likewise, true drop is an anagram of protrude

Assessment:

8 - 11	Average
12 - 17	Good
18 - 22	Very Good
23 - 25	Exceptional

Spatial Aptitude

Visual Odd One Out Test

1   A- B is a mirror image of E, C is a mirror image of D

2. D- the rest are the same figure rotated

3. B- in all the others there is a dot in either two circles or two triangles

4. C- it contains six lines, the rest contain five.

5. C- A is the same as E with black white dot reversal,
    and similarly B is the same as D

6. D- it is the only one where the black dot is the topmost dot

7. E- it spirals anti-clockwise from the centre.
    The rest spiral clockwise from the centre.

8. C- in all the others white arrows point to straight-sided figures
    and black arrows point to curved-sided figures

9. D- A is the same figure as F, B is the same figure as C,
    and G is the same figure as E

10. E- A plus D completes two concentric circles, as do B plus F and C plus G

Assessment:

4 - 5	Average
6 - 7	Good
8	Very Good
9 - 10	Exceptional

Visual Sequence Test

1. D- each circle moves from top to bottom one space at a time and each time the top space is vacated a new circle is introduced at the top.

2. B- the number of black dots is decreasing by 1 at each stage and the number of white dots is increasing by 1

3. C- there are two alternate figure sequences. The first figure rotates 90° anti-clockwise at each stage and the second figure rotates 90° clockwise

4. B- each line becomes horizontal in turn, working from top to bottom

5. A- the large arc moves 90° clockwise at each stage and the small arc moves 180°

6. B- the dot in the corner moves one corner clockwise at each stage, as does the longest line. The short line moves side, corner side etc. anti-clockwise at each stage

7. B- the black and white dots moves 45° clockwise and anti-clockwise respectively at each stage, and a new dot is added beneath them at each stage

8. C- two lines disappear, one clockwise and one anti-clockwise at each stage

9. E- the large pentagon is disappearing one line at a time at each stage, and the small pentagon is appearing one line at a time at each stage

10. C- there are four separate sequences. The top left quarter alternates white circle/black circle; the top right quarter alternates between two diagonals; the bottom left alternates white circle, white circle with inner dot, black circle; the bottom right alternates line top/middle/bottom.

Assessment:

4 -	5	Average
6 -	7	Good
	8	Very Good
9 -	10	Exceptional

Visual Analogy Test

1. F- the squares rotate 90° clockwise and join up. The cross in the centre transfers to the middle of the circle in the left hand square

2. D- the large circles turn to small circles and vice versa

3. D- the figure originally on the left goes to the top of the pyramid, the figure in the middle rotates 180° and goes bottom right, the figure on the right goes to bottom left

4. B- the dots outside the circle move from top to bottom and change from black to white or vice versa; the dots inside the circle retain their position but change from black to white and vice versa

5. B- the number of sides in the external figure increase by 1, and the number of sides in the internal figure decrease by 1

6. D- the triangle swaps places with the diamond, and the diamond rotates 90°

7. C- the circle rotates 45° anti-clockwise, and the long line moves 45° clockwise

8. C- opposite figures change places and change from black to white and vice versa

9. A- the original figure moves 180°. A second figure is also added which is 90° clockwise from the original

10. E- only black or white dots that appear in the same position twice in the preceding three squares are transferred to the final square.

Assessment:

4 -	5	Average
6 -	7	Good
	8	Very Good
9 -	10	Exceptional

Technical Aptitude

1. A and D

2. a telescope

3. C. density

4. B. ergonomics

5. the base of the wheel

6.

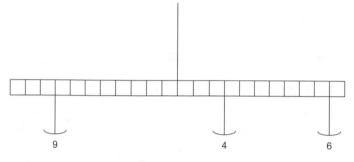

$8 \times 9 = 72$

$3 \times 4 = 12$
$10 \times 6 = \underline{60}$
72

7. C- not proven

8. wedge

9. C- parallelogram

10. 1010

11. 19

12. division sign

13. 144°

Divide the pentagon into five equal triangles.
Each angle equals 360° (a circle) / 5 = 72°
Therefore, the shaded angle = 72 x 2 = 144°

14. 152.8cm
   152.8cm = 1528mm
     200cm = 2000 mm
              <u>72</u> mm
            3600 mm

   3600 mm = 360 cm = 3.6 m

15. Until she reaches a point 600m from the fulcrum.

   50,000N x 3m (150,000) = 250N x 600m (150,000)

Assessment:

5 - 6	Average
7 - 9	Good
10 - 12	Very Good
13 - 15	Exceptional

Advanced Intelligence IQ Test

1. platitudinous, hackneyed

2. mercurial, changeable

3. b. commodity

4. noxious, inoffensive

5. erect, recumbent

6. generally

7. spontaneous

8. decision, order

9. distribution, assets

10. discount, premium

11. WV
    STuVW

12. bewilderment

13. UDFON = found

14. eminent, whose, momentous, complimented, continuous

15. F

16. double

17. R

18. university- all the others are rooms within larger buildings

19. orb- it is a sphere, all the others being spirals

20. C- looking both across and down, the first two numbers in each row and column added together produce the third number, and the second and third numbers added produce the fourth number

21. D- looking across the numbers in each line progresses by 2. Looking down they progress by 3

22. 82- deduct 3.6 each time

23.

```
      ┌────┐
      │ 23 │
   ┌──┼────┼────┐
   │ 7│ 30 │ 16 │
   └──┼────┼────┘
      │ 14 │
      └────┘
```

   7 + 16 = 23, 23 + 7 = 30, 30 - 16 = 14

24. 16 minutes

   12 noon less 16 = 11.44
   11.44 plus 4 minutes = 11.48
   11 am plus 48 minutes (16 x 3) = 11.48

25. 14
   7 x 8 / 4

26. Tony 4, Sally 12, Mary 48

27. 1226
   Take the difference between 75 and 87 (12) and 69 and 43 (26)

28. 28
   7 x 8 / 2

29. 7- add the two numbers in the same position in the first two circles to obtain the numbers in the third circle

30. C- each row and column contains the numbers 1234 once each only.

31. 3- in lines across multiply the first two numbers and divide by the third number to obtain the fourth number i.e. (9 x 2) / 6 = 3

32. 12 noon
As the faster one gains on the slower one by 5 minutes per hour, it will be exactly 1 hour ahead after 12 hours (12 x 5 = 60)

33. D- the second three squares are the same as the first three squares, but with black/white dot reversal

34. D- it is the only one where the dot is not inside the circle

35. A- all dots originally inside, move to outside, and vice versa, and change from black to white, and vice versa

36. C- looking both across and down, a circle is added to alternate squares

37. C and D- so that the dot appears in the triangle and two of the circles

38. B- so that each of the four different figures appears once in each row and column

39. E- the black dot appears in every alternate circle, the white dot appears in the first, fourth, seventh and tenth circles and the line appears in the first, fifth and ninth circles

40. B- all the rest have the same combination of white/black/black/white/white/white

---

Assessment:

Each completely correct answer scores one point

35 - 40	Exceptional
30 - 34	Excellent
23 - 29	Very Good
17 - 22	Good
10 - 16	Average

Problem Solving

1. Which is the way to your hometown?

    Then go whichever way he tells you. If he is from Shamtown he will point you in the direction of Honestville, because he always lies. If he is from Honestville he will point you to Honestville, because he always tells the truth.

2. Buy the item from the man on the next stall for £10.00 and then sell both items for £50.00 each.

3. Put three coins in each pan. If they are equal the counterfeit coin is one of the other two. In this case weigh these two coins only, to see which is the heavier.

    If at the first weighing the two sets of three coins are unequal, the counterfeit coin is in the set of three lighter coins. In this case weigh just two of these coins against each other. If they are unequal, the lighter coin is counterfeit, but if they are equal it is the third coin, the one which has not been weighed, which is counterfeit.

4. The main reason is that they are safer than square covers because they cannot fall down the hole. You could also say that they are more economical because circles cover more area using less material. They are also easier to handle because they can be rolled.

5. At 3.15 the hour hand will have moved a quarter of the distance between 3 and 4, whereas the minute hand will point directly at 3. One quarter of the distance between 3 and 4 is 1/48 (12 x 4) of the whole clock face (360°). The difference between the two hands is, therefore, 360/48 = 7.5°.

    The following are some of the questions you should be considering in respect of questions 6 and 7:

6. What is the population of Chicago? What percentage of this population is male? How many times a year does the average man get a haircut? How many haircuts a day/week does the average barber perform? How many days a week are barbers shops usually open? How often does a barber on average take a holiday?

    A similar sort of question posed by interviewers is: How many gas stations are there in the United States of America?

7. How deep is an Olympic size swimming pool? How long is it, and how wide? From this information the cubic capacity can be calculated. How big is a golf ball? What is its cubic capacity? As golf balls are round, what packing space would be wasted?

   Or:

   How many golf balls could I fit into my wash basin at home? What is the cubic capacity of my wash basin compared with an Olympic sized swimming pool?

8.

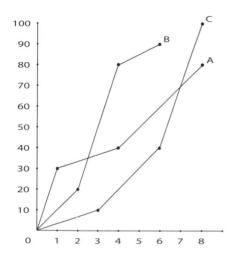

   The most efficient way of solving this problem is to create a graph to chart each traveller's progress.

   From the above it can be seen that Traveller B overtook Traveller A at approximately 2.20 pm, and Traveller C overtook traveller A at approximately 7.00 pm.

9. Train to 15-metre siding, collect coach B. Back to 15-metre siding, leave B in 5-metre siding. Back to 15-metre siding, up to top, pick up A and push down onto B in 5-metre siding. Reverse up to top with coaches A and B in tow. Drop B in its original place and come back up with A to the top. Take A to 5-metre siding and leave. Reverse to top, collect B and reverse to top. Leave B in A's original position. Reverse train and go across to 15-metre siding. Push A up to B's original position and return train to starting point.